SOPHOCLES was born near Athens around 496 B.C. and would become, along with Aeschylus and Euripides, one of the great dramatists of his age. The son of a wealthy merchant, he studied all the arts and enjoyed life as a citizen of the thriving Greek empire. An accomplished actor and innovator of theater, he is credited with writing more than 120 plays, only seven of which have survived in their entirety. Of these, OEDIPUS THE KING is generally considered the greatest. Translated into an acting version here, this classic play is given an added dimension through the clarity of its modernized prose.

This Enriched Classic edition of Sophocles' OEDIPUS THE KING is translated and introduced by Bernard Knox, director emeritus of Harvard's Center for Hellenic Studies in Washington, D.C. His books include *Oedipus at Thebes*, *The Heroic Temper*, and *Backing into the Future: The Classical Tradition and Its Renewal*. He is the editor of *The Norton Book of Classical Literature* and in 1992 was named Jefferson Lecturer in the humanities by the National Endowment for the Humanities.

TITLES AVAILABLE IN THE ENRICHED CLASSICS SERIES

OTHER WASHINGTON SQUARE PRESS CLASSICS

Oedipus the King

Sophocles

Translated and Introduced by
Bernard Knox

WASHINGTON SQUARE PRESS
PUBLISHED BY POCKET BOOKS

New York   London   Toronto   Sydney   Singapore

For orders other than by individual consumers, Pocket Books grants a discount on the purchase of **10 or more** copies of single titles for special markets or premium use. For further details, please write to the Vice President of Special Markets, Pocket Books, 1230 Avenue of the Americas, 9th Floor, New York, NY 10020-1586.

For information on how individual consumers can place orders, please write to Mail Order Department, Simon & Schuster, Inc., 100 Front Street, Riverside, NJ 08075.

 A Washington Square Press Publication of
POCKET BOOKS, a division of Simon & Schuster, Inc.
1230 Avenue of the Americas, New York, NY 10020

Translation, Introduction, Preface copyright © 1959 by Bernard M.W. Knox, copyright renewed © 1987 by Bernard M.W. Knox
Revised Introduction copyright © 1994 by Simon & Schuster, Inc.

Sophocles.
 [Oedipus Rex. English]
 Oedipus the King/Sophocles; translated and introduced by Bernard Knox.
  p. cm.
 Includes bibliographical references.
 ISBN: 0-671-88804-8
 1. Greek drama (Tragedy)–Translations into English. 2. Oedipus (Greek mythology)–Drama. I. Knox, Bernard MacGregor Walker. II. Title.
PA4414.07K6 1994   94-16222
882'.01–dc20   CIP

First Washington Square Press printing June 1972
First printing of this revised editon September 1994

20 19 18 17 16 15 14 13 12 11

WASHINGTON SQUARE PRESS and colophon are registered trademarks of Simon & Schuster, Inc.

Front cover illustration by Amy Guip

Printed in the U.S.A.

FOR BIANCA VANORDEN

CONTENTS

ANCIENT GREECE

TRANSLATOR'S PREFACE

This translation is an "acting version." It was made for those members of the Stratford Shakespearian Festival Company of Canada who performed in a series of four filmed lessons on the *Oedipus the King* of Sophocles in 1958. The films were made by the Council for a Television Course in the Humanities for Secondary Schools, and this edition of the translation was published for use by students studying the play with the aid of the films.

There are now many translations available, some of them written with performance in mind. But when the films were made, none of the existing versions met the demands of the situation. The films, which were aimed at students in their junior year of high school, required a version that would be immediately intelligible, in performance, to an audience which had had no previous acquaintance with Greek tragedy and little acquaintance with the theater in any form. The translation has to be clear, simple, direct—its only aim the creation and maintenance of dramatic excitement. To put it another way, it had to be a version which would place no obstacles between the modern audience and the dramatic power of the play.

There was one version that seemed, at first glance, to meet our needs, one by a great poet, William Butler Yeats. He had made it for performance in the Abbey Theatre in Dublin, where it was produced in 1926. We actually began our work on the films using this text, but very soon realized that we would have to abandon it. In his superb versions of the choral odes, where Yeats used verse, he sometimes indulged his own poetic obsessions and produced images and phrases that have nothing to do with Sophocles—"the Delphic Sybil's trance," for example, or "For Death is all the fashion now, till even Death be dead." And though the prose of the dialogue scenes is strong and simple—"Lady Gregory and I," he wrote, "went through it all, altering every sentence that would not be intelligible on the Blasket Islands"—here, too, we were faced with a serious problem. For reasons he did not see fit to explain, Yeats cut the play in the same high-handed way he edited Wilde's *Ballad of Reading Gaol* ("My work gave me that privilege"); what the result is in the case of Wilde I leave to others to judge, but in the case of Sophocles it is close to disastrous. In the last scene of the play, for example, he has omitted 90 of the 226 lines Sophocles wrote, and he has moved parts of speeches as much as a hundred lines away from their true position, not to mention the fact that at one point he has taken two lines from Oedipus, given them to the chorus, and slapped them into the middle of one of Oedipus' long speeches at a point where an interruption destroys the power of the speech. As if this were not enough, he has, in an earlier scene, omitted Jocasta's famous lines on chance, without which the play loses a great deal of its meaning.

So the play had to be translated again. I have used prose (though in some of the choral odes, where the words seem to fall naturally into short lines, I have printed them in that form to suggest the liturgical style of the choral performance. I do not claim that they are verse). The criteria for the prose were clarity and vigor, and in the hope of attaining these two objectives, I have sacrificed everything else. The result is not Sophocles, but I hope that it will give some impression of one dimension of the Sophoclean masterpiece—its dramatic power.

Since 1958 many new translations of the play, in both prose and verse, have made their appearance and found their readers. But the Oedipus films are still widely used in schools and, in any case, the steady demand for this version of the play warrants its reissue in a revised edition.

The text of the play is complete; the few minor omissions of words or phrases are all dictated by the canons of speed and simplicity. In the first scene, for example, Oedipus addresses Creon as "son of Menoeceus." Few people in college, let alone high school, know who Menoeceus was, and the momentary check the strange name gives the audience cuts them off for a moment from the forward movement of the play in which they should be relentlessly involved. So I have dropped Menoeceus and translated simply

"Creon." I have heard it argued that even though classical names may be unfamiliar to the modern audience they have a certain dignity and traditional familiarity which creates "atmosphere," but many years of teaching Greek tragedy in translation have convinced me that to the ordinary American student the name Menoeceus contains no more dignity than the name Lobengula, and is no more familiar; Lobengula in fact has the advantage in that he can pronounce it.

So in many other details. Apollo is sometimes called Loxias in Greek tragedy, and for the Greek poet and audience the use of one name rather than the other sometimes had a point, but actors cannot explain what the point is. In this translation Apollo is always Apollo. And the Delphic oracle is always the Delphic oracle, even if in the Greek it happens to be Pytho. Where the chorus speculates about "enmity between the Labdacids and the son of Polybus," I have translated "Laius and Oedipus." The translation aims to involve in the dramatic impetus of the play an audience which will find it hard enough to acquire even the necessary minimum of basic information. If we have to choose, and I think we do, between making students feel the excitement of the play and making sure they know who Labdacus was, I have no doubt which to choose.

The stage directions all envisage a modern production, not a reconstruction of the original performance. I have taken the liberty of adding a few remarks of a directorial nature where I thought them necessary to bring out the meaning of the passage. I have indicated my belief that the closing lines of the chorus are not part of the Sophoclean original, and at vv. 376–7 I have translated the manuscript reading, not the lines as emended by Brunck. My reasons for all this, and for many other things in the translation, will be found in my *Oedipus at Thebes* (Yale University Press, 1957).

I wish to thank Mr. Douglas Campbell, of the Stratford company, who gave me his expert (and overwhelming) advice on those parts of the translation which are used in the films, and an actress friend (who does not wish to be named) who went over every line of my text to test it for stage delivery. It is because of their patience and generosity that I have the confidence to call this translation an "acting version."

INTRODUCTION

Sophocles

Sophocles was born at Colonus, a village just outside the city of Athens, around 496 B.C. His father, Sophillos, was a wealthy man who saw to it that his son had the best teachers available—among them, a famous musician, Lampros. This would turn out to be of great importance, for the Athenian dramatist had to provide the music as well as the words for the songs of the chorus in his tragedies. The young Sophocles was chosen to lead the chorus that sang a hymn of thanksgiving to the gods for the great naval victory at Salamis, a battle fought in 480 B.C.

It was the turning point in a war that saved Greece from a large-scale Persian invasion aimed at bringing mainland Greece under Persian rule; the Greek cities of the islands and coasts of the Aegean Sea had already been annexed. In that sea battle the fleet of the democratic city-state of Athens played a decisive role, and Athens went on to lead a naval campaign which liberated the Greek cities from Persian rule. The newly freed cities joined Athens in an alliance, the Delian League, which pursued the war against Persia. But the League, in which Athens was the dominant military power, eventually became an empire: though they were still called allies, the other cities were in fact subjects, required to make financial contributions for the maintenance and operations of the Athenian fleet.

The growing power and influence of Athens aroused the fears of those cities that had been her allies in the war against the Persian invaders. Chief among them was Sparta, the city whose invincible infantry made it as formidable by land as Athens was by sea. The rest of the fifth century saw periods of war and uneasy peace between the two rivals for the hegemony of the Greek world. In 431 B.C. the final struggle, the Peloponnesian War, began. It ended twenty-seven years later, in 404, with the defeat and unconditional surrender of Athens.

Sophocles, who lived to be ninety years old, played a distinguished part in the turbulent events of the century. He served Athens often as ambassador, as general on at least one occasion, as treasurer of the Delian League, and as a member of the special commission of ten that was chosen to guide Athens through the desperate last years of the war, after the disastrous failure of an Athenian attempt to conquer the rich and far-off Greek cities in Sicily. But he did not have to witness Athens' surrender; he died in 406 B.C., in the same year as his younger rival in the theater, Euripides.

Sophocles was known to his fellow-citizens not only

as an active participant in the affairs of the democratic state, but also as the most consistently successful of the poet-dramatists who composed and directed their plays at the annual spring festival of the god Dionysus. At that festival three tragic poets, selected from applicants by a city magistrate, presented three plays each in a competition for first, second and third prizes. Sophocles won his first victory in 468 B.C., when he was twenty-eight years old; he was competing against Aeschylus, the great dramatist of the generation that had defeated the Persian invaders at Salamis.

This was the start of a career which was to bring him the first prize no less than eighteen times. He was sometimes awarded the second prize (as in the year when he produced *Oedipus the King*) but never, we are told, the third.

Sophocles wrote 123 plays. Only seven of them have come down to us complete. They are: *Ajax* (probably the earliest of the plays that have survived), *Antigone* (produced in 442 B.C.), *Oedipus the King* (probably between 429 and 420), *Philoctetes* (409), *Oedipus at Colonus* (produced after his death, in 401), and *Electra* and *Women of Trachis,* dates uncertain. Among these seven plays, *Oedipus the King* is generally regarded as the dramatic masterpiece not only of Sophocles but also of the whole magnificent range of ancient tragedy.

The City

The Athens of Sophocles was by modern standards a small and uncomfortable city. The total population of Athens and its surrounding territory, Attica, was probably not more than three hundred thousand, and the city itself was crowded, dirty and, from a material point of view, primitive—the Athenians had no running water in their houses, no central heating, no adequate artificial light. And yet it was in this city and at this time that the foundations of our modern Western civilization were firmly laid. In fifth-century Athens, European philosophy, history, drama, architecture, and sculpture emerged full-grown in masterpieces which have been dominating examples ever since.

The extraordinary achievements of fifth-century Athenians will probably never be satisfactorily explained, but there are certain historical factors which help us to understand why the human spirit was so enormously energetic and creative in this particular time and place. Early in the century (490–479 B.C.), the Greeks, weak, poor, and divided, had astonished the world (and themselves) by defeating at Salamis an invasion led by the great King of Persia himself, at the head of what must have seemed like an overwhelming force. The Greeks were inspired by a new heroic vision of their own potentialities; if they had beaten off the Persian army and fleet, there was nothing they could not do. In Athens, especially, the result of the victory was a fantastic burst of energy which showed itself not only in political and naval offensive action against Persia on its home ground, but also in every domain of civic and private endeavor.

It so happened that Athens possessed a form of government particularly adapted to encourage and guide this newfound energy. Athens was a democracy, the first in the history of the world. Its institutions allowed and even demanded a freedom of thought and discussion which was the best possible soil for the growth of new ideas, new forms of action and achievement.

It was the kind of democracy that is possible only in a relatively small community; it worked not through elected representatives, as ours does, but through an assembly of the whole citizen body, a town meeting, in fact. There was, of course, a council, which prepared the agenda for the meetings of the assembly and dealt with current business between those meetings. The members of the council, as well as the executive officers, were elected to serve for one year only. There was only one exception to this term limitation—the office of general; there were ten of them, representatives of the ten tribal regiments in which the Athenian citizens were enrolled. This was an office of vital importance; once a competent man was elected, the obvious thing to do was to keep him on the job. Pericles, the political leader of the democracy during its greatest days, was elected general year after year and from this position directed the foreign and domestic policies of Athens. But powerful and influential as he became, he still had to stand for re-election every year.

This direct democracy, with its instant control of

the executive power, had great advantages. Official corruption, for example, was almost impossible, since every magistrate, at the end of his one-year term, had to present his accounts at a public meeting, where any citizen could question him. Lobbying by vested interests was nonexistent; there were no long-term representatives to influence or bribe. The only modern equivalent would be some form of instant referendum, through which the citizen body could make its will known on any issue at once, and see the will of the majority translated into immediate action.

Even Pericles, the charismatic and successful leader of the Athenian people from mid-century until his death in 429, was subject to the wishes of the full citizen assembly and in fact, in 430 the Athenians, suffering from shortages caused by the war and, worse still, the onset of a devastating plague, did not re-elect him to the board of generals for the first time in many years. He was elected again the following year, but died of the plague.

But direct democracy had its disadvantages too. There were several occasions during the long war on which the assembly, carried away by passion and the manipulation of that passion by skillful orators, made decisions it came to regret. In 426 the rich island of Lesbos, which had been treated much more leniently than many of the other subject-allies of Athens, declared its independence and called on Athens' enemy, Sparta, for help. The rebels were finally forced to surrender, and the Athenian assembly met to decide the terms of their punishment. Fired by the speeches of a popular politician called Cleon, they decided to massacre the male population and sell the women and children into slavery; a ship was dispatched to the Athenian commander on Lesbos with those instructions. But the Athenians had second thoughts, and at a further assembly called by opponents of the original decree, they rescinded the order; the ship carrying the cancellation arrived just in time to prevent the massacre. On a later occasion the Athenians were not so lucky. In 415, at a time when the war with Sparta had reached a stalemate formalized by a truce, the assembly—dazzled by the promises of Alcibiades, a brilliant but unreliable member of the family of Pericles—embarked on a hazardous imperialist venture: the conquest of the rich Greek cities of far-off Sicily. What they clearly should have done was use the time granted by the truce to recover from the damage sustained in ten years of war, to build up their military and economic resources, but instead they "fell in love"—the only phrase the historian Thucydides could find to describe their mood—with the idea of adding Sicily to their empire. Disregarding the warnings of elder statesmen, they assembled and sent off to Sicily a huge expeditionary force; "no armament so magnificent or costly," Thucydides said, "had ever been sent out by any Greek power." The result was a stupendous disaster; not a single ship and very few of the men returned, and though the war, now renewed by Sparta, dragged on for a few more years, it could only end in Athenian defeat.

Direct democracy—the full participation of the whole citizen body in the work of government and the immediate response of elected authority to its constituents' wishes—had not only its obvious values but also its dangers. And in our own republic, in this age of instant communication, of television, telephone banks and computer networks, the possibility of "electronic democracy"—of voters' pressure bypassing those checks and balances written into the Constitution by the Founding Fathers—has added a new relevance to the study of the world's first attempt to establish "government of the people, by the people, and for the people."

In the case of Athenian democracy, however, the "people" were in fact a minority of the population. Attendance at meetings of the assembly as well as election to the council or the magistracies was open only to male Athenian citizens, men whose parents were legally married and were both citizens themselves. Women, though they were citizens, did not participate in the business of governing the city, nor did resident aliens (of whom there were a great many living in Athens) nor, of course, did the slaves.

An Athenian woman had no political rights, and in the law courts, even in cases where her property might be at issue, a male relative had to speak for her. She had only one career open to her, that of wife and mother. She would be married young, at the age of sixteen or so, to an older man, to whom she brought a dowry; the marriage would be arranged by her father or some other male relative. Once married she would spend most of her time in the house, where she would be in charge of the training and supervision of the household slaves, the care of domestic equipment and supplies, the storage and distribution of grain, olive oil, and wine, the drafting and control of the household budget, and the manufacture of clothes for the whole family, from the raw wool to the finished garment.

This situation was an inheritance from earlier times, when the individual family had to struggle for survival on a small farm in a far-from-fertile land; harsh conditions imposed a rigid division of labor, and marriage was not a matter of individual choice but a means of advancing family interests by forming alliances. But these customs still prevailed in the democratic and wealthy city of Athens, and there were some who questioned their validity. In the intellectual ferment of the last half of the century the role of women in the family and society emerged as a subject for discussion and reappraisal, and one of the places where such new ideas were expressed was the theater. In Euripides' play *Medea,* which was produced in 431 B.C., the heroine makes a long speech that expresses women's discontent with their situation. "First of all," she says, "we have to dispense large sums of money to buy a husband, to acquire a master for our body . . . and it is a critical matter whether we get a good one or a bad . . . A man, when he's tired of the people in his home, goes out . . . and turns to a companion of his own age. But we are forced to fix our gaze on one person alone. . . ." And in another play, the *Tereus* of Sophocles, a female character put the case even more forcefully. "When we are children in our father's house, our life is the most pleasant in the world; young girls grow up in thoughtless delight. But when we reach maturity and intelligence, we are expelled, bought and sold, far away from the gods of our fathers and from our parents, some to foreigners, some to houses where everything is alien, others to houses where they meet with hostility. But all this, when one night has joined us to our husband, we must accept, and pretend that all is well." Philosophers as well as dramatists discussed the issue. In the next century Plato, defending his proposal that in the ideal constitution sketched in his *Republic* women as well as men should be selected as members of the Guardians, the ruling elite, remarked that "to divide mankind into male and female for the purposes of public life or education, or anything except the begetting and bearing of children, is just as absurd as to divide it into the long-haired and the bald." And, though the Athenian democratic experiment was brought to an end by foreign intervention before such ideas could have any practical application, we should remember in this connection that our own Constitution of 1787 denied the vote to women until 1920, when the Nineteenth Amendment was passed; that England gave women the vote in 1928, and that in France women had to wait for that right until 1945.

Slaves, of course, had no rights of any kind; they were the property of their owners. There is one in *Oedipus the King,* the old shepherd who knows the secret of Oedipus' birth and who, when asked by Oedipus if he was a member of the royal household, replies, "I was. A slave. Not bought, though. I was born and reared in the palace." Most slaves in fifth-century Athens, however, were foreigners—speakers of foreign languages from the Balkans or Asia Minor captured by slavers or sold by their own people. We have no reliable statistics for the number of slaves in Athens and the territory of Attica, any more than we do for the number of resident aliens or slaves. Possible figures for the year 431 B.C., which saw the opening of the long war that was to end in the defeat of Athens and the loss of her empire, are 172,000 citizens, 30,000 resident aliens, and 110,000 slaves. The one reliable figure we have is the statement of Thucydides, who fought in the war and wrote its history, that when, after the Athenian disaster in Sicily, the Spartans set up a permanent fort on Attic territory only fourteen miles from Athens, 20,000 slaves deserted to the enemy, even though they could have had no expectation that such a move would guarantee their freedom. They were probably slaves from the silver mines, where conditions were bad enough to make them feel that any change would be for the better.

Slavery is a phenomenon for which there is no excuse and which has been mostly (though not entirely) suppressed in the modern world. But all ancient societies (like most modern societies before the industrial revolution that transformed both industry and agriculture) depended on some kind of forced labor if they were to rise above the level of rural poverty. Slavery, in Egypt as in Israel, in Greece as in Rome, was the only institution that could release the energy and intellect of the native population for the development of the skills and arts that built the great cities of Babylon, Memphis, Athens, and Rome, engineered and managed the irrigation systems that produced the abundant harvests watered by the Euphrates and the

Nile, and created the great literatures that are still a vital part of our heritage.

For Athens, at least, there is evidence that domestic slaves (unlike those who worked in the silver mines) were better treated than anywhere else in Greece. In fact the author of an anti-democratic pamphlet written sometime in the fifth century (we do not know his name) complained that in Athens slaves would not make way for you in the street and that you were not allowed to hit them. The reason for this, he added maliciously, was that since you could not tell from their appearance the difference between free men and slaves, you might beat an Athenian citizen by mistake. Slaves could be given their freedom as a reward for devotion to their duties; in fact a fourth-century Athenian treatise on household management recommends fixing a termination date for the slave's period of service. "To set the prize of freedom before him is both just and useful, since having a prize to work for, and a time defined for its award, he will put his heart into his work." There is, of course, nothing "just" about slavery, no matter how well the slave may be treated. But we should bear in mind that the development of democracy with full rights for all has been a long, slow, and painful process. It is remarkable enough that Athens invented self-rule by its male citizens many centuries before anything of the kind appeared again. And as for the slaves, we Americans can hardly afford to be too censorious about the matter, for when the great document of our own democratic faith, the Declaration of Independence, declared that "all men are created equal," the man who drafted it and many of those who signed it were owners of African slaves, an injustice that was not righted until nearly a century later, and then only at the cost of a bloody civil war.

Athenian democracy, then, was government not so much by the people as by the native, free, male citizens. But those citizens were much more active in the work of self-government than we are today. The council that watched over the city's affairs between sessions of the assembly was five hundred strong, and since membership was renewed annually, there would be few Athenians who did not serve on that important body for a year. And in the assembly he could always, if confident enough, make his voice heard; the proceedings began with a question put by a herald: "Who wishes to speak?"

In other spheres of activity, too, the Athenian acted in person rather than through representatives. In the court of law, for example, he could not hire a lawyer, (there were none) but had to state his own case before a jury of his fellow-citizens. He probably would have been very active in this sphere, for the Athenians were only too ready to sue each other. He also acted for himself in sports, which the Greeks, like us, followed with passionate interest. There were professional athletes, of course, but most of the competitors at the great Greek games—the Olympics, for example— were amateurs, ordinary citizens who had become experts in the athletic exercises which every young Athenian practiced as a matter of course.

The Athenian of Sophocles' time was thus forced, by the circumstances of his life, to act in person in many situations where today the citizen turns to the expert, and this meant that his interest in all the questions of the day was not academic, but practical and passionate. And this interest was not confined to political and economic questions. The writers, artists, and philosophers of Athens, unlike their counterparts today who appeal to a select minority, found a mass audience which was quick to react, to understand, to criticize. This may help to explain the tremendous steps forward which were taken in the arts and many other fields in Athens in the fifth century B.C.

The Theater

One of the great achievements of fifth-century Athens was the development of the theater, the first in the Western world. Its origins in Greece are lost in the dark of early history; it is doubtful that the fifth-century Athenians themselves could have explained how the theater started. But by the time of Sophocles it was a flourishing institution, an important event in the calendar of the city's communal life. We do know that it began as a dance. The oldest element in the performance was a chorus, and the chorus was a team of dancers—the Greek word *choros* means "dance," not "song," a meaning preserved in the word *choreography*. The theater began as a dance that was part of the worship of the god Dionysus; it was a ceremony of praise and prayer, performed on a circular dancing floor. It was probably a rather simple affair, like the religious dance ceremonies performed at other times and in other places—in Africa, in Australia, and in our own country by native Americans. Such dancers often wear masks, and in Athens, long after the dance of the chorus had become the theater, the dancers and the actors still wore masks.

Though dances of this type are common to many cultures all over the world, it was only in Athens that such a dance was somehow transformed into fully developed drama. How it happened we shall probably never know, but it is possible to guess. The masked chorus danced and sang, its subject some story about Dionysus. Somebody at some point added to the dance of the chorus another masked performer who did not dance or sing, but spoke, and who gave the chorus some new information or answered its questions. This was the first actor or, as the Greeks called him, *hypokrites,* a term formed from the Greek word that originally meant "to answer." The name of the experimental genius who added the first actor to the dance was, according to the Greeks, Thespis and, if he did nothing else, his name deserves to be remembered. For if one actor, why not two? And with two actors, we have the beginning of drama as we know it; the two actors can actually represent Dionysus and one of his companions, or even two characters not connected with Dionysus at all. If two actors, why not three? The dramatist who added a third actor was Sophocles himself.

In the late fifth century, when *Oedipus the King* was first produced, the theater was still a religious place, and the performance was an act of worship of the god Dionysus, the god of all living, growing things, and especially of the vine. The plays were presented at his annual festival, which took place in the early spring. In Athens you could not go to the theater whenever you wanted to; it was active only during the three-day festival of Dionysus. But when the Athenians did go to the theater, they took it seriously. They went at sunrise and sat through three tragedies, a short farcical play which had a chorus of satyrs (the half-bestial companions of Dionysus), and a comedy. They did this for three days in succession. The three tragedies and the satyr play performed on any one day were all by the same poet, though a different poet wrote the comedy. At the end of the festival, prizes were awarded by a board of judges, who would naturally take their cues from the reactions of the audience; the three tragic and the three comic poets were awarded first, second, and third prizes. The first prize was a crown of ivy. There was also a prize for best actor. The actors, highly skilled professionals, were paid by the state; they were all men, as in the theater of Shakespeare. The dramatists, too, received some compensation from the state, but we have no idea how much. The expenses of the production—the rich costumes and the training of the chorus, volunteers with some talent for singing—were shouldered by a rich private citizen, chosen for this public service by the presiding magistrate. There was a charge for admission, but it was small, and citizens who could not afford to pay it were given free tickets. The theater was not, as with us, an entertainment for the privileged few who could pay the price of admission; it was one of the privileges the democratic regime offered to all of its citizens.

The open-air theater had a seating capacity of some fourteen thousand. When the festival of Dionysus began, late in April, the audience—all those Athenians who could get away from home obligations or military service—began making its way to the theater before dawn—the old men leaning on their sticks as they walked, the soldiers from the walls, the young men from wealthy families who could afford horses to serve in the cavalry and ride in the state processions, the working population, potters, masons, farmers from just outside the city, sailors from ships in the harbor, the women who made the clothes and prepared the food for the family, the boys from the wrestling school—all of them came, bringing a cushion to sit on (marble benches seem hard after a few hours) and food to munch during the intervals between the plays, or during the plays if they weren't very exciting. They were a very lively audience, likely to burst into tears if the play was powerful and well acted, or to hiss and whistle if they didn't like it.

What they saw from their seats in the open air was not what we expect to see in the theater. From the marble benches they could see the circular dancing floor and behind it the stage building, with doors and perhaps columns, which would represent a palace or a temple and from which the masked actors would make an "entrance." There was no curtain, no lighting, no special effects; the simple scenery consisted mostly of props—a statue or an altar. A trumpet call gave the signal for silence and attention, and after it, the play began with the appearance of a masked actor or with the chorus marching past the stage building to its position on the dancing floor. The audience had no program to tell them the dramatic time and place, no list of the cast of characters. The opening lines of the play had to make clear the identity of the characters, the place and time, and the situation. This was easily and economically done, since the play was nearly always based on a story already well known to the audience; a few hints would be enough to set the stage action in the framework of the story as the audience already knew it.

The masks worn by the chorus and actors seem to have been fairly standardized. There were recognizable types—old man, middle-aged man, youth, old woman, and so on. For *Oedipus the King,* a special mask probably had to be made for the entry of Oedipus after he has put out his eyes. The masks, like all full-face masks, would naturally exaggerate the size of the face, but they were not the grotesque exaggerations sometimes pictured in handbooks and on modern theater curtains. The artificially heightened hair over the forehead which most modern reproductions show is now generally agreed to be an innovation of the Greek theater of a much later day than that of Sophocles, and the popular idea that the mouth of the mask was a funnel that acted as a megaphone has no basis in fact. The masks certainly ruled out the play of facial expression which we regard today as one of the actor's most important skills, but in the theater of Dionysus, where even the front row of spectators was sixty feet away from the stage (the back rows were three hundred feet away), facial expression could not have been seen anyway. And the masks had a practical value. They made it possible for the same actor to play two or even three or four different parts in different scenes of the play—a useful arrangement in Athens, where trained actors whose voices could reach the rear rows of the immense audience were scarce and expensive. In *Oedipus the King,* all the speaking parts were played by three actors. A probable arrangement was: one actor for Oedipus; another for the priest, Jocasta, the shepherd, and the messenger from inside the house; and the third actor for Creon, Tiresias, and the Corinthian messenger.

The dress of the actors, as we can see from contemporary vase paintings, was ornate and magnificent. But the once-popular idea that fifth-century actors wore a sort of elevator shoe that gave them abnormal height and prevented fast movement onstage is obviously mistaken. In Sophocles' last play, *Oedipus at Colonus,* for example, Antigone struggles as she is dragged offstage by Creon's guards, and in Euripides' *Helen,* the heroine runs to take sanctuary at a tomb and dodges around her pursuer to get there.

It is often stated that the fifth-century dramatists were bound by the so-called classical unities of place and time, and that they tastefully avoided blood and horror on the stage. Such ideas have no basis in fact. First, change of scene, though difficult because of the presence of the chorus, was possible in the Greek theater—the scenes are changed in the *Ajax* of Sophocles and the *Eumenides* of Aeschylus. Second, there are many places in the surviving plays where long intervals of dramatic time separate one scene from another. And last, the spectators in the theater of

Dionysus were treated to many a violent and horrific spectacle—Ajax impales himself on his sword; Philoctetes, suffering from an ulcerated foot, screams in agony, falls into delirium and finally into unconsciousness; Evadne throws herself on the burning funeral pyre of her husband; Prometheus has an iron wedge driven through his chest; and Oedipus, in our play, comes out of the palace feeling his blinded way, his face running with blood. The Athenian audience was a mass audience, and the Athenian dramatists, like Shakespeare after them, learned how to combine the subtlest poetic use of language with the unashamed exploitation of strong visual effects.

There is one aspect of the performance that remains strange to us in spite of every effort of the historical imagination; it is always the least successful feature of modern revivals of the plays. This is the chorus. Early in the play a group of twelve or fifteen masked dancers came marching out to take up their positions on the circular dancing floor in front of the stage building. They remained there until the end of the play. And at intervals during the play, usually with the stage area cleared of actors, they danced and at the same time sang, to a flute accompaniment, a choral ode. These odes were written in complicated meters and ornate, complex, lyrical language; their content was liturgical and reflective rather than dramatic. The choral odes were, like the masks, a legacy from the original form of worship out of which the drama evolved, and in the later years of the fifth century, especially in those plays of Euripides which abandoned tragic themes and concentrated on the sheer excitement of a melodramatic, romantic plot, they were treated as musical interludes between the scenes played by the actors. But Sophocles used them with the utmost poetic and dramatic skill to illustrate, discuss, and set in a broader social and religious context the actions and speeches of the characters in the play.

The choral odes in *Oedipus the King* are a brilliant example of what a dramatic genius was able to do with an obstinately undramatic form. The first chorus, a prayer to the gods, brings home to us, in a way individual actors could never do, the reality of the plague as seen through the eyes of a whole people. The second presents us with the agonized reflections of the people of Thebes on the accusations and counteraccusations of Oedipus and Tiresias; a people sits in judgment on its ruler. In the third the chorus points up and explores for us the great issue raised by the action—the truth or falsity of divine prophecy— and in closing lines full of dramatic tension takes its stand for the truth of divine prophecy and, therefore, against Oedipus and Jocasta. The fourth ode shows us the chorus in a moment of feverish excitement and exaltation as it expresses its hopes that the secret of the birth of Oedipus, soon to be revealed, will bring glory to him and to Thebes—a magnificently ironic prelude to the tremendous scene of discovery that follows. And in the last ode, facing the full and dreadful truth, the chorus presents the fate of Oedipus as an image of man's rise and fall in words which for solemn beauty and terrifying grandeur have few equals in European literature.

INTRODUCTION

The Legend and the Play

Sophocles and his fellow dramatists used for their plays stories of a time long past which were the familiar heritage of all Athenians—stories they had learned from their parents and would pass on to their children in turn. To a large extent, then, the element of novelty, which is characteristic of the modern theater, was missing, though the stories were so rich in variants and so flexible in detail that minor surprises were possible and were often provided. But what the dramatist lost in novelty he gained in other ways. The myths he used gave to his plays, without any effort on his part, some of those larger dimensions of authority which the modern dramatist must create out of nothing if his play is to be more than a passing entertainment. The myths had the authority of history, for myth is in one of its aspects the *only* history of an age that kept no records. They had also the authority inherent in moral and religious symbols, for the myths served as typical patterns of the conduct of man and the manifestation of the gods. They were stories in which the historical, moral, and religious experience of the whole race was distilled.

The myths gave the ancient dramatist another advantage. One of the most difficult problems facing the modern dramatist—exposition, the indication early in the play of the background of the characters and their situation—was, for the ancient dramatist, no problem at all. He had only to indicate the identity of the characters and the point in the story where his play began, and the job was done. He could limit his exposition to emphasizing those particular details of the background which were important for his own treatment of the story.

The audience, once it recognized the story, knew what had preceded the action of the play. But it knew even more. It knew more or less accurately what was going to happen in the play itself. And this fact enabled the ancient dramatist to work in a vein which is characteristic of Greek tragedy and especially of Sophocles—dramatic irony. Everything said by the characters in the play means more to the audience than it does to the speaker. For the audience knows more than he does, knows the truth about the past (which Oedipus, for example, does not know) and the truth about the future. The audience during the play is in fact in the position of the gods, and is able to see the struggles, hopes, and fears of the characters against a background of the truth—past, present, and future. This situation gives to the dramatic action as a whole an intensity and complication which are the hallmark of Greek tragedy; the audience understands everything on two different levels at once. It is involved emotionally in the blind heroic efforts of Oedipus, a man like each of them; and it is detached from those efforts by its superior knowledge, the knowledge of the gods. Ancient tragedy gives the spectator an image of his own life, not only as he sees it and lives it himself, but as it must look to the all-seeing eye of divine knowledge.

This somber irony shows itself not only in the larger frame of the action but in details, too. One speech after another in the play uses the audience's knowledge to provide a dramatic shock: Jocasta's speech to Oedipus on her first entrance, with its scolding, nagging tone that suggests a mother reproving a wayward son; the answer of the chorus to the Corinthian messenger, "This lady is . . . his wife and mother of his children"; Oedipus' statement that he will fight on behalf of Laius "as if he were my own father"—all these dramatic hammer blows are made possible by the fact that the audience knows the story to begin with.

The story is old, strange, and terrible. Laius and Jocasta, the childless king and queen of Thebes, were told by the god Apollo that their son would kill his father and marry his mother. A son was born to them, and they tried to make sure that the prophecy would not come true. Laius drove a metal pin through the infant's ankles and gave it to a shepherd, with instructions to leave it to die of exposure on the nearby mountain, Cithaeron. The shepherd took the child up to the mountain, but pitied it and gave it to a fellow shepherd he met there, who came from Corinth, on the other side of the mountain range. This shepherd took the child with him and gave it to the childless king and queen of Corinth, Polybus and Merope. They brought the child up as their own son, and named him Oedipus, which in its Greek form *Oidipous* means "swollen foot" (his feet had been injured by the metal pin). So Oedipus grew up in Corinth as the king's son, with no idea of his real parentage. And Laius and Jocasta believed that their child was dead and the prophecy of Apollo false.

After Oedipus became a young man, he was told, by

a man who had drunk too much at a banquet, that he was not the real son of Polybus. He was reassured by Polybus and Merope, but a lingering doubt remained and rumors were spreading abroad. He went, on his own initiative, to Delphi, in the north of Greece, to the oracle of Apollo, to ask the god who his parents were. All he was told was that he would kill his father and marry his mother. He resolved never to return to Corinth, to Polybus and Merope, and started out to make a new life for himself elsewhere. He came to a place where three main roads met, and in the narrow place was ordered off the road and then attacked by the driver of a chariot in which an old man was riding. A fight started, and Oedipus, in self-defense, killed the old man and his attendants—all except one, who escaped and took the news to Thebes. The old man in the chariot was Laius, king of Thebes. And so the first half of the prophecy of Apollo was fulfilled. Oedipus, though he did not know it, had killed his father.

Oedipus continued on his way and came to Thebes. He found the city in distress. A monster, the Sphinx— part bird, part lion, part woman—was killing the young men of Thebes and refused to go away until someone answered her riddle. Many had tried, but all failed, and met their death. The Thebans offered a great reward to anyone who could answer the riddle of the Sphinx—the throne of Thebes and the hand of Jocasta, the widowed queen, in marriage. Oedipus volunteered to answer the riddle: "There is a creature two-footed, and also four-footed, and three-footed. It has one voice. When it goes on most feet, then it goes most slowly." Oedipus answered the riddle correctly.

The answer is Man, who goes on all fours as a child, on two feet as an adult, and on three as an old man, since he has a stick to help him along.

Oedipus married Jocasta and became king of Thebes. The prophecy was fulfilled, but he did not realize it. For many years he ruled Thebes well, an admired and just king. He had two daughters and two sons. And then a plague broke out in Thebes. The people of the city died, the cattle died, the crops rotted. The Thebans thronged the temples, and a delegation of priests went to the palace to beg Oedipus to save them. These are the priests who come onstage at the beginning of the play, and as they enter, the stage door opens and a masked actor comes out and addresses them. The play has begun.

Bernard Knox

Oedipus the King

THE CHARACTERS
in the order of their appearance

◇◇◇◇◇◇◇◇◇◇◇◇◇◇◇◇◇◇◇◇◇◇◇◇

OEDIPUS, King of Thebes

A PRIEST of Zeus

CREON, brother of Jocasta

A CHORUS of Theban citizens

TIRESIAS, a blind prophet

JOCASTA, the queen, wife of Oedipus

A MESSENGER from Corinth

A SHEPHERD

A MESSENGER from inside the palace

ANTIGONE
ISMENE } daughters of Oedipus and Jocasta

OEDIPUS THE KING

◈◈◈◈◈◈◈

*The background is the front wall of a building,
with a double door in the center. Steps lead
down from the door to stage level. In front
of the steps, in the center, a square stone altar.*

◈◈◈◈◈◈◈

[*Enter, from the side, a procession of priests and
citizens. They carry olive branches which have tufts
of wool tied on them. They lay these branches on
the altar, then sit on the ground in front of it. The
door opens. Enter Oedipus.*]

OEDIPUS

My sons! Newest generation of this ancient city
of Thebes! Why are you here? Why are you seated
there at the altar, with these branches of supplication?

The city is filled with the smoke of burning incense, with hymns to the healing god, with laments for the dead. I did not think it right, my children, to hear reports of this from others. Here I am, myself, world-famous Oedipus.

You, old man, speak up—you are the man to speak for the others. In what mood are you sitting there—in fear or resignation? You may count on me; I am ready to do anything to help. I would be insensitive to pain, if I felt no pity for my people seated here.

PRIEST

Oedipus, ruler of Thebes, you see us here at your altar, men of all ages—some not yet strong enough to fly far from the nest, others heavy with age, priests, of Zeus in my case, and these are picked men from the city's youth. The rest of the Thebans, carrying boughs like us, are sitting in the market place, at the two temples of Athena, and at the prophetic fire of Apollo near the river Ismenus.

You can see for yourself—the city is like a ship rolling dangerously; it has lost the power to right itself and raise its head up out of the waves of death. Thebes is dying. There is a blight on the crops of the land, on the ranging herds of cattle, on the still-born labor of our women. The fever-god swoops down on us, hateful plague, he hounds the city and empties the houses of Thebes. The black god of death is made rich with wailing and funeral laments.

It is not because we regard you as equal to the gods that we sit here in supplication, these children and I; in our judgment you are first of men, both in the normal crises of human life and in relations with the gods.

You came to us once and liberated our city, you freed us from the tribute which we paid that cruel singer, the Sphinx. You did this with no extra knowledge you got from us, you had no training for the task, but, so it is said and we believe, it was with divine support that you restored our city to life. And now, Oedipus, power to whom all men turn, we beg you, all of us here, in supplication—find some relief for us! Perhaps you have heard some divine voice, or have knowledge from some human source. You are a man of experience, the kind whose plans result in effective action. Noblest of men, we beg you, save this city. You must take thought for your reputation. Thebes now calls you its savior because of the energy you displayed once before. Let us not remember your reign as a time when we stood upright only to fall again. Set us firmly on our feet. You brought us good fortune then, with favorable signs from heaven—be now the equal of the man you were. You are king; if you are to rule Thebes, you must have an inhabited city, not a desert waste. A walled city or a ship abandoned, without men living together inside it, is nothing at all.

OEDIPUS

My children, I am filled with pity. I knew what you were longing for when you came here. I know only too well that you are all sick—but sick though you may be, there is not one of you as sick as I. *Your* pain torments each one of you, alone, by himself—by my spirit within me mourns for the city, and myself, and all of you. You see then, I was no dreamer you awoke from sleep. I have wept many tears, as you must know, and in my ceaseless reflection I have followed many paths of thought. My search has found one way to treat our disease—and I have acted already. I have sent Creon, my brother-in-law, to the prophetic oracle of Apollo, to find out by what action or speech, if any, I may rescue Thebes. I am anxious now when I count the days since he left; I wonder what he is doing. He has been away longer than one would expect, longer than he should be. But when he comes, at that moment I would be a vile object if I did not do whatever the god prescribes.

PRIEST

Just as you say these words, these men have signaled to me to announce Creon's arrival.

[*Enter Creon, from side.*]

OEDIPUS

[*Turns to the altar*] O King Apollo! May Creon bring us good fortune and rescue, bright as the expression I see on his face.

PRIEST

I guess that his news is joyful. For on his head is a crown of laurel in bloom.

OEDIPUS

No more guessing—soon we shall know. For he is near enough to hear us now.

[*Raising his voice*] Lord Creon, what statement do you bring us from the god Apollo?

5

CREON

Good news. For, as I see it, even things hard to bear, if they should turn out right in the end, would be good fortune.

OEDIPUS

What exactly did the god say? *Your* words inspire neither confidence nor fear.

CREON

If you wish to hear my report in the presence of these people [*Points to priests*] I am ready. Or shall we go inside?

OEDIPUS

Speak out, before all of us. The sorrows of my people here mean more to me than any fear I may have for my own life.

CREON

Very well. Here is what I was told by the god Apollo. He ordered us, in clear terms, to drive out the thing that defiles this land, which we, he says, have fed and cherished. We must not let it grow so far that it is beyond cure.

OEDIPUS

What is the nature of our misfortune? How are we to rid ourselves of it—by what rites?

CREON

Banishment—or repaying blood with blood. We must atone for a murder which brings this plague-storm on the city.

OEDIPUS

Whose murder? Who is the man whose death Apollo lays to our charge?

CREON

The ruler of this land, my lord, was called Laius. That was before *you* took the helm of state.

OEDIPUS

I know—at least I have heard so. I never saw the man.

CREON

It is to *his* death that Apollo's command clearly refers. We must punish those who killed him—whoever they may be.

OEDIPUS

But where on earth are they? The track of this ancient guilt is hard to detect; how shall we find it now?

CREON

Here in Thebes, Apollo said. What is searched for can be caught. What is neglected escapes.

OEDIPUS

Where did Laius meet his death? In his palace, in the countryside, or on some foreign soil?

CREON

He left Thebes to consult the oracle, so he announced. But he never returned to his home.

OEDIPUS

And no messenger came back? No fellow traveler who saw what happened?

CREON

No, they were all killed—except for one, who ran away in terror. But he could give no clear account of what he saw—except one thing.

8

OEDIPUS

And what was that? One thing might be the clue to knowledge of many more—if we could get even a slight basis for hope.

CREON

Laius was killed, he said, not by one man, but by a strong and numerous band of robbers.

OEDIPUS

But how could a *robber* reach such a pitch of daring—to kill a king? Unless there had been words —and money—passed between him and someone here in Thebes.

CREON

We thought of that, too. But the death of Laius left us helpless and leaderless in our trouble—

OEDIPUS

Trouble? What kind of trouble could be big enough to prevent a full investigation? Your *king* had been killed.

9

CREON

The Sphinx with her riddling songs forced us to give up the mystery and think about more urgent matters.

OEDIPUS

But I will begin afresh. I will bring it all to light. You have done well, Creon, and Apollo has, too, to show this solicitude for the murdered man. Now you will have *me* on your side, as is only right. I shall be the defender of Thebes, and Apollo's champion, too. I shall rid us of this pollution, not for the sake of a distant relative, but for my own sake. For whoever killed Laius might decide to raise his hand against me. So, acting on behalf of Laius, I benefit myself, too.

[*To priests*] Quickly, my children, as fast as you can, stand up from the steps and take these branches of supplication off the altar.

[*To guards*] One of you summon the people of Thebes here.

I shall leave nothing undone. With God's help we shall prove fortunate—or fall.

10

PRIEST

My sons, stand up. [*The priests rise.*] King Oedipus has volunteered to do what we came to ask. May Apollo, who sent the message from his oracle, come as our savior, and put an end to the plague.

[*The priests take the olive branches off the altar and exeunt to side. Oedipus goes back through the palace doors. Enter, from side, the chorus. They are fifteen dancers, representing old men. They stand for the people of Thebes, whom Oedipus has just summoned. They chant in unison the following lines, which, in the original Greek, make great use of solemn, traditional formulas of prayer to the gods.*]

CHORUS

Sweet message of Zeus! You have come from Apollo's golden temple to splendid Thebes, bringing us news. My fearful heart is stretched on the rack and shudders in terror.

Hail Apollo, Lord of Delos, healer! I worship and revere you. What new form of atonement will you demand? Or will it be some ancient ceremony, repeated often as the seasons come round? Tell me, daughter of golden Hope, immortal Voice of Apollo.

First I call upon you, immortal Athena, daughter of Zeus. And on your sister Artemis, the protector of this land, who sits in glory on her throne in the market place. And I call on far-shooting Apollo, the archer. Trinity of Defenders against Death, appear to me! If ever in time past, when destruction threatened our city, you kept the flame of pain out of our borders, come now also.

There is no way to count the pains we suffer. All our people are sick. There is no sword of thought which will protect us. The fruits of our famous land do not ripen. Our women cannot ease their labor pains by giving birth. One after another you can see our people speed like winged birds, faster than irresistible fire, to the shore of evening, to death. The city is dying, the deaths cannot be counted. The children lie unburied, unmourned, spreading death. Wives and gray-haired mothers come from all over the city, wailing they come to the altar steps to pray for release from pain and sorrow. The hymn to the Healer flashes out, and with it, accompanied by flutes, the mourning for the dead. Golden daughter of Zeus, Athena, send help and bring us joy.

I pray that the raging War-god, who now without shield and armor hems me in with shouting and burns me, I pray that he may turn back and leave the borders of this land. Let him go to the great sea gulf of the Western ocean or north to the Thracian coasts which give no shelter from the sea. For now, what the night spares, he comes for by day.

Father Zeus, you that in majesty govern the blazing lightning, destroy him beneath your thunderbolt!

Apollo, king and protector! I pray for the arrows from your golden bow—let them be ranged on my side to help me. And with them the flaming torches of Artemis, with which she speeds along the Eastern mountains. And I invoke the god with the golden headdress, who gave this land his name, wine-faced Dionysus, who runs with the maddened girls—let him come to my side, shining with his blazing pine-torch, to fight the god who is without honor among all other gods.

[*The chorus stays on stage. Enter Oedipus, from the palace doors. He addresses the chorus—the people of Thebes.*]

OEDIPUS

You are praying. As for your prayers, if you are willing to hear and accept what I say now and so treat the disease, you will find rescue and relief from distress. I shall make a proclamation, speaking as one who has no connection with this affair, nor with the murder. Even if I had been here at the time, I could not have followed the track very far without some clue. As it is, I became a Theban citizen with you after it happened. So I now proclaim to all of you, citizens of Thebes: whoever among you knows by whose hand Laius son of Labdacus was killed, I order him to reveal the whole truth to me.

If he is afraid to speak up, I order him to speak even against himself, and so escape the indictment, for he will suffer no unpleasant consequence except exile; he can leave Thebes unharmed.

[*Silence while Oedipus waits for a reply.*]

Secondly, if anyone knows the identity of the murderer, and that he is a foreigner, from another land, let him speak up. I shall make it profitable for him, and he will have my gratitude, too.

[*Pause.*]

14

But if you keep silent—if someone among you refuses my offer, shielding some relative or friend, or himself—now, listen to what I intend to do in that case. That man, whoever he may be, I banish from this land where I sit on the throne and hold the power; no one shall take him in or speak to him. He is forbidden communion in prayers or offerings to the gods, or in holy water. Everyone is to expel him from their homes as if he were himself the source of infection which Apollo's oracle has just made known to me. That is how I fulfill my obligations as an ally to the god and to the murdered man. As for the murderer himself, I call down a curse on him, whether that unknown figure be one man or one among many. May he drag out an evil death-in-life in misery. And further, I pronounce a curse on myself if the murderer should, with my knowledge, share my house; in that case may I be subject to all the curses I have just called down on these people here. I order you all to obey these commands in full for my sake, for Apollo's sake, and for the sake of this land, withering away in famine, abandoned by heaven.

Even if this action had not been urged by the god, it was not proper for you to have left the matter unsolved—the death of a good man and a

king. You should have investigated it. But now I am
in command. I hold the office he once held, the
wife who once was his is now mine, the mother of
my children. Laius and I would be closely connected by children from the same wife, if his line
had not met with disaster. But chance swooped
down on his life. So I shall fight for him, as if he
were my own father. I shall shrink from nothing in
my search to find the murderer of Laius, of the
royal line of Thebes, stretching back through Labdacus, Polydorus and Cadmus, to ancient Agenor.
On those who do not co-operate with these measures
I call down this curse in the gods' name: let no
crop grow out of the earth for them, their wives
bear no children. Rather let them be destroyed by
the present plague, or something even worse. But
to you people of Thebes who approve of my action
I say this: May justice be our ally and all the gods
be with us forever!

CHORUS

[*One member of the chorus speaks for them all.*]

You have put me under a curse, King, and under
the threat of that curse I shall make my statement.
I did not kill Laius and I am not in a position to
say who did. This search to find the murderer

should have been undertaken by Apollo who sent the message which began it.

OEDIPUS

What you say is just. But to compel the gods to act against their will—no man could do that.

CHORUS LEADER

Then let me make a second suggestion.

OEDIPUS

And a third, if you like—speak up.

CHORUS LEADER

The man who sees most eye to eye with Lord Apollo is Tiresias and from him you might learn most clearly the truth for which you are searching.

OEDIPUS

I did not leave *that* undone either. I have already sent for him, at Creon's suggestion. I have sent for him twice, in fact, and have been wondering for some time why he is not yet here.

17

CHORUS LEADER

Apart from what he will say, there is nothing but old, faint rumors.

OEDIPUS

What were they? I want to examine every single word.

CHORUS LEADER

Laius was killed, so they say, by some travelers.

OEDIPUS

I heard that, too. Where is the man who saw it?

CHORUS LEADER

If he has any trace of fear in him, he won't stand firm when he hears the curses you have called down on him.

OEDIPUS

If he didn't shrink from the action he won't be frightened by a word.

18

CHORUS LEADER

But here comes the one who will convict him. These men are bringing the holy prophet of the gods, the only man in whom truth is inborn.

[*Enter Tiresias, from the side. He has a boy to lead him, and is accompanied by guards.*]

OEDIPUS

Tiresias, you who understand all things—those which can be taught and those which may not be mentioned, things in the heavens and things which walk the earth! You cannot see, but you understand the city's distress, the disease from which it is suffering. You, my lord, are our shield against it, our savior, the only one we have. You may not have heard the news from the messengers. We sent to Apollo and he sent us back this answer: relief from this disease would come to us only if we discovered the identity of the murderers of Laius and then either killed them or banished them from Thebes. Do not begrudge us your knowledge—any voice from the birds or any other way of prophecy you have. Save yourself and this city, save me, from all the infection caused by the dead man. We are in your hands. And the noblest of labors is for a man to help his fellow men with all he has and can do.

TIRESIAS

Wisdom is a dreadful thing when it brings no profit to its possessor. I knew all this well, but forgot. Otherwise I would never have come here.

OEDIPUS

What is the matter? Why this despairing mood?

TIRESIAS

Dismiss me, send me home. That will be the easiest way for both of us to bear our burden.

OEDIPUS

What you propose is unlawful—and unfriendly to this city which raised you. You are withholding information.

TIRESIAS

I do not see that your talking is to the point. And I don't want the same thing to happen to me.

20

OEDIPUS

If you know something, in God's name, do not turn your back on us. Look. All of us here, on our knees, beseech you.

TIRESIAS

You are all ignorant. I will never reveal my dreadful secrets, or rather, yours.

OEDIPUS

What do you say? You know something? And will not speak? You intend to betray us, do you, and wreck the state?

TIRESIAS

I will not cause pain to myself or to you. Why do you question me? It is useless. You will get nothing from me.

OEDIPUS

You scoundrel! You would enrage a lifeless stone. Will nothing move you? Speak out and make an end of it.

21

TIRESIAS

You blame my temper, but you are not aware
of one *you* live with.

OEDIPUS

[*To chorus*]

Who could control his anger listening to talk
like this—these insults to Thebes?

TIRESIAS

What is to come will come, even if I shroud it
in silence.

OEDIPUS

What is to come, *that* is what you are bound to
tell *me*.

TIRESIAS

I will say no more. Do what you like—rage at
me in the wildest anger you can muster.

OEDIPUS

I will. I am angry enough to speak out. I understand it all. Listen to me. I think that *you* helped

22

to plan the murder of Laius—yes, and short of actually raising your hand against him you did it. If you weren't blind, I'd say that you alone struck him down.

TIRESIAS

Is that what you say? I charge you now to carry out the articles of the proclamation you made. From now on do not presume to speak to me or to any of these people. *You* are the murderer, *you* are the unholy defilement of this land.

OEDIPUS

Have you no shame? To start up such a story! Do you think you will get away with this?

TIRESIAS

Yes. The truth with all its strength is in me.

OEDIPUS

Who taught you this lesson? You didn't learn it from your prophet's trade.

TIRESIAS

You did. I was unwilling to speak but you drove me to it.

23

OEDIPUS

What was it you said? I want to understand it clearly.

TIRESIAS

Didn't you understand it the first time? Aren't you just trying to trip me up?

OEDIPUS

No, I did not grasp it fully. Repeat your statement.

TIRESIAS

I say that you are the murderer you are searching for.

OEDIPUS

Do you think you can say that twice and not pay for it?

TIRESIAS

Shall I say something more, to make you angrier still?

24

OEDIPUS

Say what you like. It will all be meaningless.

TIRESIAS

I say that without knowing it you are living in shameful intimacy with your nearest and dearest. You do not see the evil in which you live.

OEDIPUS

Do you think you can go on like this with impunity forever?

TIRESIAS

Yes, if the truth has power.

OEDIPUS

It has, except for you. You have no power or truth. You are blind, your ears and mind as well as eyes.

TIRESIAS

You are a pitiful figure. These reproaches you fling at me, all these people here will fling them at you—and before very long.

OEDIPUS

[*Contemptuously*]

You live your life in one continuous night of darkness. Neither I nor any other man that can see would do you any harm.

TIRESIAS

It is not destiny that I should fall through you. Apollo is enough for that. It is *his* concern.

OEDIPUS

Was it Creon, or you, that invented this story?

TIRESIAS

It is not Creon who harms you—you harm yourself.

OEDIPUS

Wealth, absolute power, skill surpassing skill in the competition of life—what envy is your reward! For the sake of this power which Thebes entrusted to me—I did not ask for it—to win this power faithful Creon, my friend from the beginning, sneaks up on me treacherously, longing to drive me out. He sets this intriguing magician on me, a lying quack, keen sighted for what he can make, but blind in prophecy.

[*To Tiresias*] Tell me, when were you a true prophet? When the Sphinx chanted her riddle here, did *you* come forward to speak the word that would liberate the people of this town? That riddle was not for anyone who came along to answer—it called for prophetic insight. But you didn't come forward, you offered no answer told you by the birds or the gods. No. *I* came, know-nothing Oedipus, *I* stopped the Sphinx. I answered the riddle with my own intelligence—the birds had nothing to teach me. And now you try to drive me out, you think you will stand beside Creon's throne. I tell you, you will pay in tears for this witch-hunting—you and Creon, the man that organized this conspiracy. If you weren't an old man, you would already have realized, in suffering, what your schemes lead to.

CHORUS LEADER

If we may make a suggestion—both his words and yours, Oedipus, seem to have been spoken in anger. This sort of talk is not what we need—what we must think of is how to solve the problem set by the god's oracle.

TIRESIAS

King though you are, you must treat me as your equal in one respect—the right to reply. That is a power which belongs to me, too. I am not your servant, but Apollo's. I am not inscribed on the records as a dependent of Creon, with no right to speak in person. I can speak, and here is what I have to say. You have mocked at my blindness, but you, who have eyes, cannot see the evil in which you stand; you cannot see where you are living, nor with whom you share your house. Do you even know who your parents are? Without knowing it, you are the enemy of your own flesh and blood, the dead below and the living here above. The double-edged curse of your mother and father, moving on dread feet, shall one day drive you from this land. You see straight now but then you will see darkness. You will scream aloud on that day; there is no place which shall not hear you, no part of Mount Cithaeron here which will not ring in echo, on that day when you know the truth about your wedding, that evil harbor into which you sailed before a fair wind.

There is a multitude of other horrors which you do not even suspect, and they will equate you to yourself and to your own children. There! Now smear me and Creon with your accusations. There is no man alive whose ruin will be more pitiful than yours.

OEDIPUS

Enough! I won't listen to this sort of talk from you. Damn you! My curse on you! Get out of here, quickly. Away from this house, back to where you came from!

TIRESIAS

I would never have come here if you had not summoned me.

OEDIPUS

I didn't know that you were going to speak like a fool—or it would have been a long time before I summoned you to my palace.

TIRESIAS

I am what I am—a fool to you, so it seems, but the parents who brought you into the world thought me sensible enough. [*Tiresias turns to go.*]

OEDIPUS

Whom do you mean? Wait! Who is my father?

TIRESIAS

This present day will give you birth and death.

OEDIPUS

Everything you say is the same—riddles, obscurities.

TIRESIAS

Aren't you the best man alive at guessing riddles?

OEDIPUS

Insult me, go on—but that, you will find, is what makes me great.

TIRESIAS

Yet that good fortune was your destruction.

OEDIPUS

What does that matter, if I saved Thebes?

TIRESIAS

I will go, then. Boy, lead me away.

OEDIPUS

Yes, take him away. While you're here you are a hindrance, a nuisance; once out of the way you won't annoy me any more.

TIRESIAS

I am going. But first I will say what I came here to say. I have no fear of you. You cannot destroy me. Listen to me now. The man you are trying to find, with your threatening proclamations, the murderer of Laius, that man is here in Thebes. He is apparently an immigrant of foreign birth, but he will be revealed as a native-born Theban. He will take no pleasure in that revelation. Blind instead of seeing, beggar instead of rich, he will make his way to foreign soil, feeling his way with a stick. He will be revealed as brother and father of the children with whom he now lives, the son and husband of the woman who gave him birth, the murderer and marriage-partner of his father. Go think this out. And if you find that I am wrong, then say I have no skill in prophecy.

[*Exit Tiresias led by boy to side. Oedipus goes back into the palace.*]

CHORUS

Who is the man denounced by the prophetic voice from Delphi's cliffs—the man whose blood-stained hands committed a nameless crime? Now is the time for him to run, faster than storm-swift

31

horses. In full armor Apollo son of Zeus leaps upon him, with the fire of the lightning. And in the murderer's track follow dreadful unfailing spirits of vengeance.

The word of Apollo has blazed out from snowy Parnassus for all to see. Track down the unknown murderer by every means. He roams under cover of the wild forest, among caves and rocks, like a wild bull, wretched, cut off from mankind, his feet in pain. He turns his back on the prophecies delivered at the world's center, but they, alive forever, hover round him.

The wise prophet's words have brought me terror and confusion. I cannot agree with him, nor speak against him. I do not know what to say. I waver in hope and fear; I cannot see forward or back. What cause for quarrel was there between Oedipus and Laius? I never heard of one in time past; I know of none now.

I see no reason to attack the great fame of Oedipus in order to avenge the mysterious murder of Laius.

Zeus and Apollo, it is true, understand and know in full the events of man's life. But whether a mere man knows the truth—whether a human prophet knows more than I do—who is to be a fair judge of that? It is true that one man may be wiser than another. But I, for my part, will never join those who blame Oedipus, until I see these charges proved. We all saw how the Sphinx came against him—there his wisdom was proved. In that hour of danger he was the joy of Thebes. Remembering that day, my heart will never judge him guilty of evil action.

[*Enter Creon, from side.*]

CREON

Fellow citizens of Thebes, I am here in an angry mood. I hear that King Oedipus brings terrible charges against me. If, in the present dangerous situation, he thinks that I have injured him in any way, by word or deed, let me not live out the rest of my days with such a reputation. The damage done to me by such a report is no simple thing—it is the worst there is—to be called a traitor in the city, by all of you, by my friends.

CHORUS LEADER

This attack on you must have been forced out of him by anger; he lost control of himself.

CREON

Who told him that *I* advised Tiresias to make these false statements?

CHORUS LEADER

That's what was said—but I don't know what the intention was.

CREON

Were his eyes and mind unclouded when he made this charge against me?

CHORUS LEADER

I don't know. It is no use asking *me* about the actions of those who rule Thebes. Here is Oedipus. Look, he is coming out of the palace.

[*Enter Oedipus, from door.*]

OEDIPUS

[*To Creon*]

You! What are you doing here? Do you have the face to come to my palace—you who are convicted as my murderer, exposed as a robber attempting to steal my throne? In God's name, tell me, what did you take me for when you made this plot—a coward? Or a fool? Did you think I wouldn't notice this conspiracy of yours creeping up on me in the dark? That once I saw it, I wouldn't defend myself? Don't you see that your plan is foolish—to hunt for a crown without numbers or friends behind you? A crown is won by numbers and money.

CREON

I have a suggestion. You in your turn listen to a reply as long as your speech, and, after you have heard me, *then* judge me.

OEDIPUS

You are a clever speaker, but I am a slow learner—from *you*. I have found you an enemy and a burden to me.

CREON

Just one thing, just listen to what I say.

OEDIPUS

Just one thing, don't try to tell me you are not a traitor.

35

CREON

Listen, if you think stubbornness deprived of intelligence is a worth-while possession, you are out of your mind.

OEDIPUS

Listen, if you think you can injure a close relative and then not pay for it, you are out of your mind.

CREON

All right, that's fair. But at least explain to me what I am supposed to have done.

OEDIPUS

Did you or did you not persuade me that I ought to send for that "holy" prophet?

CREON

Yes, I did, and I am still of the same mind.

OEDIPUS

Well then, how long is it since Laius . . . [*Pause.*]
36

CREON

Did what? I don't follow your drift.

OEDIPUS

Disappeared, vanished, violently murdered?

CREON

Many years ago; it is a long count back in time.

OEDIPUS

And at that time, was this prophet at his trade?

CREON

Yes, wise as he is now, and honored then as now.

OEDIPUS

Did he mention my name at that time?

CREON

No, at least not in my presence.

OEDIPUS

You investigated the murder of Laius, didn't you?

37

CREON

We did what we could, of course. But we learned nothing.

OEDIPUS

How was it that this wise prophet did not say all this *then?*

CREON

I don't know. And when I don't understand, *I* keep silent.

OEDIPUS

Here's something you *do* know, and could say, too, if you were a loyal man.

CREON

What do you mean? If I know, I will not refuse to answer.

OEDIPUS

Just this. If he had not come to an agreement with you, Tiresias would never have called the murder of Laius *my* work.

CREON

If that's what he says—you are the one to know. Now I claim my rights from you—answer my questions as I did yours just now.

OEDIPUS

Ask your questions. I shall not be proved a murderer.

CREON

You are married to my sister, are you not?

OEDIPUS

The answer to that question is yes.

CREON

And you rule Thebes jointly and equally with her?

OEDIPUS

She gets from me whatever she wants.

CREON

And I am on an equal basis with the two of you, isn't that right?

OEDIPUS

Yes, it is, and that fact shows what a disloyal friend you are.

CREON

No, not if you look at it rationally, as I am explaining it to you. Consider this point first—do you think anyone would prefer to be supreme ruler and live in fear rather than to sleep soundly at night and still have the same power as the king? I am not the man to long for royalty rather than royal power, and anyone who has any sense agrees with me. As it is now, I have everything I want from you, and nothing to fear; but if I were king, I would have to do many things I have no mind to. How could the throne seem more desirable to me than power and authority which bring me no trouble? I can see clearly—all I want is what is pleasant and profitable at the same time. As it is now, I am greeted by all, everyone salutes me, all those who want something from you play up to me —that's the key to success for them. What makes you think I would give up all this and accept what you have? No, a mind which sees things clearly, as I do, would never turn traitor. I have never been tempted by such an idea, and I would never have put up with anyone who took such action.

You can test the truth of what I say. Go to Delphi and ask for the text of the oracle, to see if I gave you an accurate report. One thing more. If you find that I conspired with the prophet Tiresias, then condemn me to death, not by a single vote, but by a double, yours and mine both. But do not accuse me in isolation, on private, baseless fancy. It is not justice to make the mistake of taking bad men for good, or good for bad. To reject a good friend is the equivalent of throwing away one's own dear life—that's my opinion. Given time you will realize all this without fail: time alone reveals the just man —the unjust you can recognize in one short day.

CHORUS LEADER

That is good advice, my lord, for anyone who wants to avoid mistakes. Quick decisions are not the safest.

OEDIPUS

When a plotter moves against me in speed and secrecy, then I too must be quick to counterplot. If I take my time and wait, then his cause is won, and mine lost.

CREON

What do you want then? Surely you don't mean to banish me from Thebes?

OEDIPUS

Not at all. Death is what I want for you, not exile.

CREON

You give a clear example of what it is to feel hate and envy.

OEDIPUS

You don't believe me, eh? You won't give way?

CREON

No, for I can see you don't know what you are doing.

OEDIPUS

Looking after my own interests.

CREON

And what about mine?

A bronze sculpture of the head of Sophocles. (COPYRIGHT BRITISH MUSEUM)

Vase painting, detail, of a Greek warrior attacking a
Persian invader.

The god Dionysus, detail from a vase painting. It was the annual spring festival of Dionysus for which Sophocles wrote his plays. In *Oedipus the King* the chorus invokes "the god with the golden headdress, who gave this land his name, wine-faced Dionysus . . ."

A Grecian woman of the noble class. In the time of Sophocles, women had no political rights, although the role of women in the family and society emerged as a subject for public discussion; one such forum was the theater. *(COSTUMES OF THE GREEKS AND ROMANS, THOMAS HOPE, DOVER PUBLICATIONS, INC., 1962)*

An interior of a regal Grecian home. *(PICTURE COLLECTION DIVISION OF THE NEW YORK PUBLIC LIBRARY)*

A Greek chariot, drawn from a vase painting.

A bronze statuette of a dancer; the Greek theater had its origins in dance.

An aerial view of the fourth century B.C. theater at
Epidaurus. (NICOS KONTOS, GREEK TOURIST OFFICE)

A seat from the theater of Dionysus in Athens. (GREEK TOURIST OFFICE)

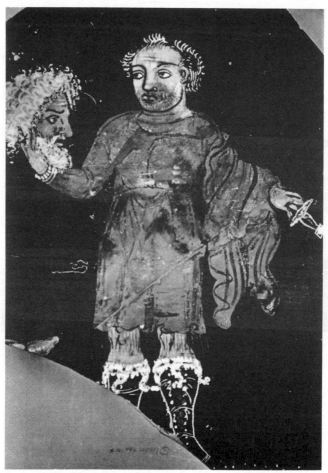

An actor holding his mask of an old man, from a vase fragment. (GREEK TOURIST OFFICE)

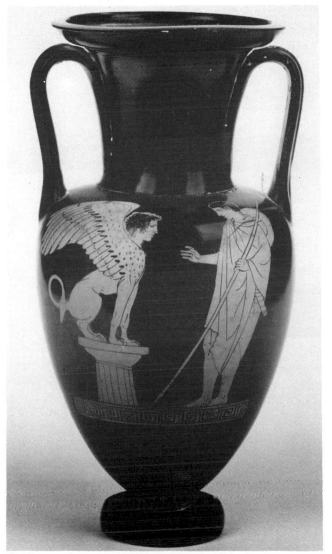

Oedipus solving the riddle of the Sphinx, from a vase painting. (COURTESY, MUSEUM OF FINE ARTS, BOSTON)

A sketch of the cliffs at Delphi. It was the oracle of Apollo at Delphi which told Oedipus that he would kill his father and marry his mother, and to which he sends Creon to ask for help to save Thebes from the plague.

A model of the Parthenon. A temple to Athena, the
Parthenon was built in Athens in the fifth century B.C.

A model of the interior of the Parthenon, showing how the colossal statue of Athena, the goddess of wisdom, skills, and warfare, may have appeared. The original statue was made of ivory and gold.

A typical chorus in a Greek theater. (PICTURE COLLECTION DIVISION OF THE NEW YORK PUBLIC LIBRARY)

A marble head of Zeus. "Father Zeus, you that in majesty govern the blazing lightning . . ." says the chorus, representing the people of Thebes, in this play. (COURTESY, MUSEUM OF FINE ARTS, BOSTON)

A silver coin of Greece, 530–490 B.C. This coin depicts the head of Athena on one side, and on the reverse, the owl of Athens. (COURTESY, MUSEUM OF FINE ARTS, BOSTON)

A vase painting depicting the birth of Athena who, according to Greek legend, sprang forth, fully formed, from Zeus's head. The chorus appeals to the "Golden daughter of Zeus, Athena," to "send help and bring us joy." (COURTESY, MUSEUM OF FINE ARTS, BOSTON)

Apollo and Artemis, shown in a vase painting. Again,
the chorus appeals to the gods for help: "Apollo, king
and protector! I pray for the arrows from your golden
bow . . . And with them the flaming torches of
Artemis." Apollo was the god of music, poetry,
prophecy, and medicine; Artemis was his twin sister and
the goddess of the moon, wild animals, and hunting.

A Greek woman unfastening the pins on her garment; it is such pins that Oedipus uses to blind himself. "He ripped out the golden pins with which her clothes were fastened, raised them high above his head, and speared the pupils of his eyes. 'You will not see,' he said, 'the horrors I have suffered and done.'" *(COSTUMES OF THE GREEKS AND ROMANS,* THOMAS HOPE, DOVER PUBLICATIONS, INC., 1962)

OEDIPUS

You are a born traitor.

CREON

And you don't understand anything.

OEDIPUS

Whether I do or not—I am in power here.

CREON

Not if you rule badly.

OEDIPUS

[*To Chorus*]

Listen to him, Thebes, my city.

CREON

My city, too, not yours alone.

CHORUS LEADER

Stop, my lords. Here comes Jocasta from the house, in the nick of time. With her help, you must compose this quarrel between you.

43

[*Enter Jocasta, from door.*]

JOCASTA

Have you no sense, God help you, raising your voices in strife like this? Have you no sense of shame? The land is plague-stricken and you pursue private quarrels. [*To Oedipus*] You go into the house, and you, too, Creon, inside. Don't make so much trouble over some small annoyance.

CREON

Sister, your husband, Oedipus, claims the right to inflict dreadful punishments on me. He will choose between banishing me from my fatherland and killing me.

OEDIPUS

Exactly. Jocasta, I caught him in a treacherous plot against my life.

CREON

May I never enjoy life, but perish under a curse, if I have done to you any of the things you charge me with.

44

JOCASTA

In God's name, Oedipus, believe what he says.
Show respect for the oath he swore by the gods—
do it for my sake and the sake of these people here.

CHORUS

Listen to her, King Oedipus. Think over your
decision, take her advice, I beg you.

OEDIPUS

What concession do you want me to make?

CHORUS

Creon was no fool before, and now his oath in-
creases his stature. Respect him.

OEDIPUS

Do you know what you are asking?

CHORUS

Yes, I know.

OEDIPUS

Tell me what it means, then.

45

CHORUS

This man is your friend—he has sworn an oath—don't throw him out dishonored on the strength of hearsay alone.

OEDIPUS

Understand this. If that is what you are after, you want me to be killed or banished from this land.

CHORUS

No. By the sun, foremost of all the gods! May I perish miserably abandoned by man and God, if any such thought is in my mind. My heart is racked with pain for the dying land of Thebes—must you add new sorrows of your own making to those we already have?

OEDIPUS

Well then, let him go—even if it *does* lead to my death or inglorious banishment. It is *your* piteous speech that rouses my compassion—not what *he* says. As for him, I shall hate him, wherever he goes.

CREON

You show your sulky temper in giving way, just as you did in your ferocious anger. Natures like

46

yours are hardest to bear for their owners—and justly so.

OEDIPUS

Get out, will you? Out!

CREON

I am going. I found you ignorant—but these men think I am right.

[*Exit Creon to side.*]

CHORUS

[*To Jocasta*]

Lady, why don't you get him into the house quickly?

JOCASTA

I will—when I have found out what happened here.

CHORUS

There was some ignorant talk based on hearsay and some hurt caused by injustice.

47

JOCASTA

On both sides?

CHORUS

Yes.

JOCASTA

And what did they say?

CHORUS

Enough, that is enough, it seems to me. I speak in the interests of the whole country. Let this matter lie where they left it.

OEDIPUS

You see where your good intentions have brought you. This is the result of turning aside and blunting the edge of my anger.

CHORUS

My king, I said it before, more than once—listen to me. I would be exposed as a madman, useless, brainless, if I were to turn my back on you. You found Thebes laboring in a sea of trouble, you righted her and set her on a fair course. All I wish now is that you should guide us as well as you did then.

JOCASTA

In God's name, explain to me, my lord—what was it made you so angry?

OEDIPUS

I will tell you. I have more respect for you than for these people here. Creon and his conspiracy against me, that's what made me angry.

JOCASTA

Tell me clearly, what was the quarrel between you?

OEDIPUS

He says that *I* am the murderer of Laius.

JOCASTA

On what evidence? His own knowledge, or hearsay?

49

OEDIPUS

Oh, he keeps his own lips clear of responsibility
—he sent a swindling prophet in to speak for him.

JOCASTA

A prophet? In that case, rid your mind of your
fear, and listen to me. I can teach you something.
There is no human being born that is endowed with
prophetic power. I can prove it to you—and in a
few words.

A prophecy came to Laius once—I won't say
from Apollo himself, but from his priests. It said
that Laius was fated to die by the hand of his son,
a son to be born to him and to me. Well, Laius, so the
story goes, was killed by foreign robbers at a place
where three highways meet. As for the son—three
days after his birth Laius fastened his ankles together and had him cast away on the pathless
mountains.

So, in this case, Apollo did not make the son kill
his father or Laius die by his own son's hand, as he
had feared. Yet these were the definite statements of
the prophetic voices. Don't pay any attention to
prophecies. If God seeks or needs anything, he will
easily make it clear to us himself.

OEDIPUS

Jocasta, something I heard you say has disturbed me to the soul, unhinged my mind.

JOCASTA

What do you mean? What was it that alarmed you so?

OEDIPUS

I thought I heard you say that Laius was killed at a place where three highways meet.

JOCASTA

Yes, that's what the story was—and still is.

OEDIPUS

Where is the place where this thing happened?

JOCASTA

The country is called Phocis: two roads, one from Delphi and one from Daulia, come together and form one.

51

OEDIPUS

When did it happen? How long ago?

JOCASTA

We heard the news here in Thebes just before you appeared and became King.

OEDIPUS

O God, what have you planned to do to me?

JOCASTA

What is it, Oedipus, which haunts your spirit so?

OEDIPUS

No questions, not yet. Laius—tell me what he looked like, how old he was.

JOCASTA

He was a big man—his hair had just begun to turn white. And he had more or less the same build as you.

OEDIPUS

O God! I think I have just called down on myself a dreadful curse—not knowing what I did.

JOCASTA

What do you mean? To look at you makes me
shudder, my lord.

OEDIPUS

I am dreadfully afraid the blind prophet could
see. But tell me one more thing that will throw
light on this.

JOCASTA

I am afraid. But ask your question; I will answer
if I can.

OEDIPUS

Was Laius poorly attended, or did he have a
big bodyguard, like a king?

JOCASTA

There were five men in his party. One of them
was a herald. And there was one wagon—Laius was
riding in it.

OEDIPUS

Oh, it is all clear as daylight now. Who was it told you all this at the time?

JOCASTA

A slave from the royal household. He was the only one who came back.

OEDIPUS

Is he by any chance in the palace now?

JOCASTA

No, he is not. When he came back and saw you ruling in place of Laius, he seized my hand and begged me to send him to work in the country, to the pastures, to the flocks, as far away as I could —out of sight of Thebes. And I sent him. Though he was a slave he deserved this favor from me—and much more.

OEDIPUS

Can I get him back here, in haste?

JOCASTA

It can be done. But why are you so intent on this?

OEDIPUS

I am afraid, Jocasta, that I have said too much—that's why I want to see this man.

JOCASTA

Well, he shall come. But I have a right, it seems to me, to know what it is that torments you so.

OEDIPUS

So you shall. Since I am so full of dreadful expectation, I shall hold nothing back from you. Who else should I speak to, who means more to me than you, in this time of trouble?

My father was Polybus, a Dorian, and my mother Merope, of Corinth. I was regarded as the greatest man in that city until something happened to me quite by chance, a strange thing, but not worth all the attention I paid it. A man at the banquet table, who had had too much to drink, told me, over his wine, that I was not the true son of my father. I was furious, but, hard though it was, I con-

olled my feelings, for that day at least. On the
:xt day I went to my parents and questioned them.
hey were enraged against the man who had so
taunted me. So I took comfort from their attitude,
but still the thing tormented me—for the story
spread far and wide. Without telling my parents,
I set off on a journey to the oracle of Apollo, at
Delphi. Apollo sent me away with my question
unanswered but he foretold a dreadful, calamitous
future for me—to lie with my mother and beget
children men's eyes would not bear the sight of—
and to be the killer of the father that gave me life.

When I heard that, I ran away. From that point
on I measured the distance to the land of Corinth
by the stars. I was running to a place where I would
never see that shameful prophecy come true. On
my way I came to the place in which you say this
king, Laius, met his death.

I will tell you the truth, all of it. As I journeyed
on I came near to this triple crossroad and there I
was met by a herald and a man riding on a horse-
drawn wagon, just as you described it. The driver,
and the old man himself, tried to push me off the
road. In anger I struck the driver as he tried to
crowd me off. When the old man saw me coming
past the wheels he aimed at my head with a two-

pronged goad, and hit me. I paid him back in full, with interest: in no time at all he was hit by the stick I held in my hand and rolled backwards from the center of the wagon. I killed the whole lot of them.

Now, if this stranger had anything to do with Laius—is there a more unhappy man alive than I? Who could be more hateful to the gods than I am? No foreigner or citizen may take me into his house, no one can talk to me—everyone must expel me from his home. And the man who called down these curses on me was I myself, no one else. With these hands that killed him I defile the dead man's marriage bed. How can I deny that I am vile, utterly unclean? I must be banished from Thebes, and then I may not even see my own parents or set foot on my own fatherland—or else I am doomed to marry my own mother and kill my father Polybus, who brought me up and gave me life. I am the victim of some harsh divinity; what other explanation can there be?

Let it not happen, not that, I beg you, holy majesty of God, may I never see that day! May I disappear from among men without trace before I see such a stain of misfortune come upon me!

CHORUS LEADER

My lord, this makes us tremble. But do not despair—you have still to hear the story from the eyewitness.

OEDIPUS

That's right. That's my hope now, such as it is—to wait for the shepherd.

JOCASTA

Why all this urgency about his coming?

OEDIPUS

I'll tell you. If it turns out that he tells the same story as you—then I, at least, will be cleared of responsibility.

JOCASTA

What was so important in what you heard from me?

OEDIPUS

You said his story was that *several* robbers killed Laius. Well, if he speaks of the same number as you—then I am not the killer. For one could

58

never be equal to many. But if he speaks of one man alone—then clearly the balance tips towards me as the killer.

JOCASTA

You can be sure that his account was made public just as I told it to you; he cannot go back on it, the whole city heard it, not I alone. But, my lord, even if he should depart from his former account in some particular, he still would never make the death of Laius what it was supposed to be—for Apollo said clearly that Laius was to be killed by my son. But that poor infant never killed Laius; it met its own death first. So much for prophecy. For all it can say, I would not, from now on, so much as look to right or left.

OEDIPUS

Yes, I agree. But all the same, that shepherd— send someone to fetch him. Do it at once.

JOCASTA

I shall send immediately. And now let us go in. I would not do anything except what pleases you.

[*Exeunt Oedipus and Jocasta through doors.*]

CHORUS

[*Chanting in unison*]

May Destiny be with me always;
Let me observe reverence and purity
In word and deed.
Laws that stand above have been established—
Born in the upper air on high;
Their only father is heaven;
No mortal nature, no man gave them birth.
They never forget, or sleep.
In them God is great, and He does not grow
    old.

The despot is the child of violent pride,
Pride that vainly stuffs itself
With food unseasonable, unfit,
Climbs to the highest rim
And then plunges sheer down into defeat
Where its feet are of no use.
Yet I pray to God to spare that vigor
Which benefits the state.
God is my protector, on Him I shall never cease
    to call.

The man who goes his way
Overbearing in word and deed,
Who fears no justice,
Honors no temples of the gods—
May an evil destiny seize him
And punish his ill-starred pride.
How shall such a man defend his life
Against God's arrows?
If such deeds as this are honored,
Why should we join the sacred dance and wor-
  ship?

I shall go no more in reverence to Delphi,
The holy center of the earth,
Nor to any temple in the world,
Unless these prophecies come true,
For all men to point at in wonder.
O Zeus, King of heaven, ruler of all,
If you deserve this name,
Do not let your everlasting power be deceived,
Do not forget.
The old prophecies about Laius are failing,
Men reject them now.
Apollo is without honor everywhere.
The gods are defeated.

61

[*Enter Jocasta, with branches of olive.*]

JOCASTA

[*To chorus*]

Lords of Thebes, it occurred to me to come to the temples of the gods bearing in my hands these branches and offerings of incense. For Oedipus is distracted with sorrows of all kinds. He does not act like a man in control of his reason, judging the present by the past—he is at the mercy of anyone who speaks to him, especially one who speaks of terrors. I have given him advice, but it does no good. [*Facing the altar*] So I come to you, Lord Apollo, for you are closest to hand. I come in supplication with these emblems of prayer. Deliver us, make us free and clear of defilement. We are all afraid, like passengers on a ship who see their pilot crazed with fear.

[*Enter from side Corinthian messenger.*]

CORINTHIAN MESSENGER

[*To chorus*]

Strangers, can one of you tell me—where is the palace of King Oedipus? Better still, if you know, where is the king himself?

CHORUS LEADER

This is his palace, and he is inside, stranger. This lady is his queen, his wife and mother of his children.

CORINTHIAN MESSENGER

Greetings to the noble wife of Oedipus! May you and all your family be blessed forever.

JOCASTA

The same blessings on you, stranger, for your kind words. But tell us what you want. Why have you come? Have you some news for us?

CORINTHIAN MESSENGER

Good news for your house and your husband, lady.

JOCASTA

What news? Who sent you?

CORINTHIAN MESSENGER

I come from Corinth. My message will bring you joy—no doubt of that—but sorrow, too.

JOCASTA

What is it? How can it work both ways?

CORINTHIAN MESSENGER

The people of Corinth will make Oedipus their king, so I heard there.

JOCASTA

What? Is old Polybus no longer on the throne?

CORINTHIAN MESSENGER

No. He is dead and in his grave.

JOCASTA

What did you say? Polybus is dead? Dead?

CORINTHIAN MESSENGER

Condemn me to death if I am not telling the truth.

JOCASTA

[*To servant*]

You there, go in quickly and tell your master.

O prophecies of the gods, where are you now?

64

Polybus was the man Oedipus feared he might kill
—and so avoided him all this time. And now he's
dead—a natural death, and not by the hand of Oedipus.

[*Enter Oedipus, from doors.*]

OEDIPUS

Jocasta, why did you send for me to come out
here?

JOCASTA

Listen to what this man says, and see what has
become of the holy prophecies of the gods.

OEDIPUS

Who is he? What does he have to say to me?

JOCASTA

He's from Corinth. He came to tell you that
your father Polybus is dead and gone.

OEDIPUS

Is this true? Tell me yourself.

65

CORINTHIAN MESSENGER

If that's what you want to hear first, here it is,
a plain statement: Polybus is dead and gone.

OEDIPUS

How? Killed by a traitor, or wasted by disease?

CORINTHIAN MESSENGER

He was old. It did not take much to put him to
sleep.

OEDIPUS

By disease, then—that's how he died?

CORINTHIAN MESSENGER

Yes, that, and the length of years he had lived.

OEDIPUS

So! Why then, Jocasta, should we study Apollo's
oracle, or gaze at the birds screaming over our heads
—those prophets who announced that I would kill
my father? He's dead, buried, below ground. And
here I am in Thebes—I did not put hand to sword.

Perhaps he died from longing to see me again.

66

That way, it could be said that I was the cause of his death. But there he lies, dead, taking with him all these prophecies I feared—they are worth nothing!

JOCASTA

Is that not what I told you?

OEDIPUS

It is. But I was led astray by fear.

JOCASTA

Now rid your heart of fear forever.

OEDIPUS

No, I must still fear—and who would not?—a marriage with my mother.

JOCASTA

Fear? Why should man fear? His life is governed by the operations of chance. Nothing can be clearly foreseen. The best way to live is by hit and miss, as best you can. Don't be afraid that you may marry your mother. Many a man before you, in dreams, has shared his mother's bed. But to live at ease one must attach no importance to such things.

OEDIPUS

All that you have said would be fine—if my mother were not still alive. But she is, and no matter how good a case you make, I am still a prey to fear.

JOCASTA

But your father's death—that much at least is a great blessing.

OEDIPUS

Yes, I see that. But my mother, as long as she is alive, fills me with fear.

CORINTHIAN MESSENGER

Who is this woman that inspires such fear in you?

OEDIPUS

Merope, old man, the wife of Polybus.

CORINTHIAN MESSENGER

And what is there about her which frightens you?

68

OEDIPUS

A dreadful prophecy sent by the gods.

CORINTHIAN MESSENGER

Can you tell me what it is? Or is it forbidden for others to know?

OEDIPUS

Yes, I can tell you. Apollo once announced that I am destined to mate with my mother, and shed my father's blood with my own hand. That is why for so many years I have lived far away from Corinth. It has turned out well—but still, there's nothing sweeter than the sight of one's parents.

CORINTHIAN MESSENGER

Is that it? It was in fear of this that you banished yourself from Corinth?

OEDIPUS

Yes. I did not want to be my father's murderer.

CORINTHIAN MESSENGER

My lord, I do not know why I have not already

released you from that fear. I came here to bring you good news.

OEDIPUS

If you can do that, you will be handsomely rewarded.

CORINTHIAN MESSENGER

Yes, that was why I came, to bring you home to Corinth, and be rewarded for it.

OEDIPUS

I will never go to the city where my parents live.

CORINTHIAN MESSENGER

My son, it is clear that you don't know what you are doing.

OEDIPUS

What do you mean, old man? In God's name, explain yourself.

CORINTHIAN MESSENGER

You don't know what you are doing, if you are afraid to come home because of *them.*

OEDIPUS

I am afraid that Apollo's prophecy may come true.

CORINTHIAN MESSENGER

That you will be stained with guilt through your parents?

OEDIPUS

Yes, that's it, old man, that's the fear which pursues me always.

CORINTHIAN MESSENGER

In reality, you have nothing to fear.

OEDIPUS

Nothing? How, if I am the son of Polybus and Merope?

CORINTHIAN MESSENGER

Because Polybus was not related to you in any way.

OEDIPUS

What do you mean? Was Polybus not my father?

CORINTHIAN MESSENGER

No more than I am—he was as much your father as I.

OEDIPUS

How can my father be on the same level as you who are nothing to me?

CORINTHIAN MESSENGER

Because he was no more your father than I am.

OEDIPUS

Then why did he call me his son?

CORINTHIAN MESSENGER

He took you from my hands—I gave you to him.

72

OEDIPUS

Took me from your hands? Then how could he love me so much?

CORINTHIAN MESSENGER

He had been childless, that was why he loved you.

OEDIPUS

You gave me to him? Did you . . . buy me? or find me somewhere?

CORINTHIAN MESSENGER

I found you in the shady valleys of Mount Cithaeron.

OEDIPUS

What were you doing there?

CORINTHIAN MESSENGER

Watching over my flocks on the mountainside.

OEDIPUS

A shepherd, were you? A wandering day laborer?

CORINTHIAN MESSENGER

Yes, but at that moment I was your savior.

OEDIPUS

When you picked me up, was I in pain?

CORINTHIAN MESSENGER

Your ankles would bear witness on that point.

OEDIPUS

Oh, why do you speak of that old affliction?

CORINTHIAN MESSENGER

You had your ankles pinned together, and I freed you.

OEDIPUS

It is a dreadful mark of shame I have borne since childhood.

CORINTHIAN MESSENGER

From that misfortune comes the name which you still bear. *

---

* His name, Oedipus, means, in Greek, "swollen foot."

OEDIPUS

In God's name, who did it? My mother, or my father? Speak.

CORINTHIAN MESSENGER

I don't know. The one who gave you to me is the man to ask, not me.

OEDIPUS

You got me from someone else—you did not find me yourself?

CORINTHIAN MESSENGER

No. Another shepherd gave you to me.

OEDIPUS

Who was he? Do you know? Could you describe him?

CORINTHIAN MESSENGER

I think he belonged to the household of Laius.

OEDIPUS

You mean the man who was once king of this country?

CORINTHIAN MESSENGER

Yes. He was one of the shepherds of Laius.

OEDIPUS

Is he still alive? Can I talk to him?

CORINTHIAN MESSENGER

[*To chorus*]

You people who live here would know that better than I.

OEDIPUS

[*To chorus*]

Is there any one of you people here who knows this shepherd he mentioned? Has anyone seen him in the fields, or here in Thebes?

CHORUS LEADER

I think it is the same man from the fields you wanted to see before. But the queen here, Jocasta, could tell you that.

OEDIPUS

Jocasta, do you remember the man we sent for just now? Is *that* the man he is talking about?

76

JOCASTA

Why ask who he means? Don't pay any attention to him. Don't even think about what he said —it makes no sense.

OEDIPUS

What? With a clue like this? Give up the search? Fail to solve the mystery of my birth? Never!

JOCASTA

In God's name, if you place any value on your life, don't pursue the search. It is enough that *I* am sick to death.

OEDIPUS

You have nothing to be afraid of. Even if my mother turns out to be a slave, and I a slave for three generations back, *your* noble birth will not be called in question.

JOCASTA

Take my advice, I beg you—do not go on with it.

OEDIPUS

Nothing will move me. I *will* find out the whole truth.

77

JOCASTA

It is good advice I am giving you—I am thinking of you.

OEDIPUS

That "good advice" of yours is trying my patience.

JOCASTA

Ill-fated man. May you never find out who you are!

OEDIPUS

[*To attendants*]

One of you go and get that shepherd, bring him here. We will leave *her* to pride herself on her royal birth.

JOCASTA

Unfortunate! That is the only name I can call you by now. I shall not call your name again—ever!

[*Exit Jocasta to palace.*]

[*A long silence.*]

78

CHORUS

Why has the queen gone, Oedipus, why has she rushed away in such wild grief? I am afraid that from this silence evil will burst out.

OEDIPUS

Burst out what will! I shall know my origin, mean though it be. Jocasta perhaps—she is proud, *like* a woman—feels shame at the low circumstances of my birth. But I count myself the son of Good Chance, the giver of success—I shall not be dishonored. Chance is my mother. My brothers are the months which have made me sometimes small and sometimes great. Such is my lineage and I shall not betray it. I will not give up the search for the truth about my birth.

[*Exit Oedipus to palace.*]

CHORUS

[*Chanting in unison*]

If I am a true prophet
And see clear in my mind,
Tomorrow at the full moon
Oedipus will honor Mount Cithaeron
As his nurse and mother.

79

Mount Cithaeron—our king's Theban birthplace!
We shall celebrate it in dance and song—
A place loved by our king.
Lord Apollo, may this find favor in your sight.

Who was it, Oedipus my son, who bore you?
Which of the nymphs that live so long
Was the bride of Pan the mountain god?
Was your mother the bride of Apollo himself?
He loves the upland pastures.
Or was Hermes your father?
Perhaps Dionysus who lives on the mountain
    peaks
Received you as a welcome gift
From one of the nymphs of Helicon,
His companions in sport.

[*Enter from side the shepherd, accompanied by
two guards.*]

[*Enter Oedipus, from doors.*]

OEDIPUS

I never met the man, but, if I may make a guess,
I think this man I see is the shepherd we have been
looking for all this time. His age corresponds to that
of the Corinthian here, and, in any case, the men
bringing him are my servants, I recognize them.

[*To chorus leader*] You have seen the shepherd before, you should know better than I.

CHORUS LEADER

Yes, I recognize him. He was in the household of Laius—a devoted servant, and a shepherd.

OEDIPUS

I question you first—you, the stranger from Corinth. Is this the man you spoke of?

CORINTHIAN MESSENGER

This is the man.

OEDIPUS

[*To shepherd*]

You, old man, come here. Look me in the face. Answer my questions. Were you a servant of Laius once?

SHEPHERD

I was. A slave. Not bought, though. I was born and reared in the palace.

OEDIPUS

What was your work? How did you earn your living?

SHEPHERD

For most of my life I have followed where the sheep flocks went.

OEDIPUS

And where did you graze your sheep most of the time?

SHEPHERD

Well, there was Mount Cithaeron, and all the country round it.

OEDIPUS

Do you know this man here? Did you ever see him before?

SHEPHERD

Which man do you mean? What would he be doing there?

82

OEDIPUS

This one, here. Did you ever come across him?

SHEPHERD

I can't say, right away. Give me time. I don't remember.

CORINTHIAN MESSENGER

No wonder he doesn't remember, master. He forgets, but I'll remind him, and make it clear. I am sure he knows very well how the two of us grazed our flocks on Cithaeron—he had two and I only one—we were together three whole summers, from spring until the rising of Arcturus in the fall. When winter came I used to herd my sheep back to their winter huts, and he took his back to the farms belonging to Laius. Do you remember any of this? Isn't that what happened?

SHEPHERD

What you say is true, but it was a long time ago.

CORINTHIAN MESSENGER

Well, then, tell me this. Do you remember giving me a child, a boy, for me to bring up as my own?

83

SHEPHERD

What are you talking about? Why do you ask that question?

CORINTHIAN MESSENGER

Oedipus here, my good man, Oedipus and that child are one and the same.

SHEPHERD

Damn you! Shut your mouth. Keep quiet!

OEDIPUS

Old man, don't you correct *him*. It is you and your tongue that need correction.

SHEPHERD

What have I done wrong, noble master?

OEDIPUS

You refuse to answer his question about the child.

SHEPHERD

That's because he does not know what he's talking about—he is just wasting your time.

OEDIPUS

If you won't speak willingly, we shall see if pain can make you speak.

[*The guards seize the shepherd.*]

SHEPHERD

In God's name, don't! Don't torture me. I am an old man.

OEDIPUS

One of you twist his arms behind his back, quickly!

SHEPHERD

Oh, God, what for? What more do you want to know?

OEDIPUS

Did you give him the child he asked about?

SHEPHERD

Yes, I did. And I wish I had died that day.

OEDIPUS

You will die now, if you don't give an honest answer.

85

SHEPHERD

And if I speak, I shall be even worse off.

OEDIPUS

[*To guards*]

What? More delay?

SHEPHERD

No! No! I said it before—I gave him the child.

OEDIPUS

Where did *you* get it? Was it yours? Or did it belong to someone else?

SHEPHERD

It wasn't mine. Someone gave it to me.

OEDIPUS

Which of these Thebans here? From whose house did it come?

SHEPHERD

In God's name, master, don't ask any more questions.

86

OEDIPUS

You are a dead man if I have to ask you again.

SHEPHERD

It was a child born in the house of Laius.

OEDIPUS

Was it a slave? Or a member of the royal family?

SHEPHERD

Oh, God, here comes the dreadful truth. And I must speak.

OEDIPUS

And I must hear it. But hear it I will.

SHEPHERD

It was the son of Laius, so I was told. But the lady inside there, your wife, she is the one to tell you.

OEDIPUS

Did *she* give it to you?

87

SHEPHERD

Yes, my lord, she did.

OEDIPUS

For what purpose?

SHEPHERD

To destroy it.

OEDIPUS

Her own child?

SHEPHERD

She was afraid of dreadful prophecies.

OEDIPUS

What were they?

SHEPHERD

The child would kill its parents, that was the story.

88

OEDIPUS

Then why did you give it to this old man here?

SHEPHERD

In pity, master. I thought he would take it away to a foreign country—to the place he came from. If you are the man he says you are, you were born the most unfortunate of men.

OEDIPUS

O God! It has all come true. Light, let this be the last time I see you. I stand revealed—born in shame, married in shame, an unnatural murderer.

[*Exit Oedipus into palace.*]

[*Exeunt others at sides.*]

CHORUS

O generations of mortal men,
I add up the total of your lives
And find it equal to nothing.
What man wins more happiness
Than a mere appearance which quickly fades
    away?
With your example before me,

Your life, your destiny, miserable Oedipus,
    I call no man happy.

Oedipus outranged all others
And won complete prosperity and happiness.
He destroyed the Sphinx, that maiden
With curved claws and riddling songs,
And rose up like a towered wall against death—
Oedipus, savior of our city.
From that time on you were called King,
You were honored above all men,
Ruling over great Thebes.

And now—is there a man whose story is more
    pitiful?
His life is lived in merciless calamity and pain—
A complete reversal from his happy state.
O Oedipus, famous king,
You whom the same great harbor sheltered
As child and father both,
How could the furrows which your father
    plowed
Bear *you* in silence for so long?

Time, which sees all things, has found you out;
It sits in judgment on the unnatural marriage
Which was both begetter and begot.

O son of Laius,
I wish I had never seen you.
I weep, like a man wailing for the dead.
This is the truth:
You returned me to life once
And now you have closed my eyes in darkness.

[*Enter, from the palace, a messenger.*]

MESSENGER

Citizens of Thebes, you who are most honored in this city! What dreadful things you will see and hear! What a cry of sorrow you will raise, if, as true Thebans, you have any feeling for the royal house. Not even the great rivers of Ister and Phasis could wash this house clean of the horrors it hides within. And it will soon expose them to the light of day—horrors deliberately willed, not involuntary. Those calamities we inflict on ourselves are those which cause the most pain.

CHORUS LEADER

The horrors we knew about before were burden enough. What other dreadful news do you bring?

MESSENGER

Here is the thing quickest for me to say and you to hear. Jocasta, our queen, is dead.

CHORUS LEADER

Poor lady. From what cause?

MESSENGER

By her own hand. You are spared the worst of what has happened—you were not there to see it. But as far as my memory serves, you shall hear the full story of that unhappy woman's sufferings.

She came in through the door in a fury of passion and rushed straight towards her marriage bed, tearing at her hair with both hands. Into her bedroom she went, and slammed the doors behind her. She was calling the name of Laius, so long dead, remembering the child she bore to him so long ago—the child by whose hand Laius was to die, and leave her, its mother, to bear monstrous children to her own son. She wailed in mourning for her marriage, in which she had borne double offspring, a husband from her husband and children from her child. And after that—but I do not know exactly how she died. For Oedipus came bursting in, shouting, and so we could not watch Jocasta's suffering to the end; all of us looked at him as he ran to and fro. He rushed from one of us to the other, asking us to give him a sword, to tell him where he could find his wife—no, not his wife, but his mother, his mother and the mother of his children.

It must have been some supernatural being that showed the raving man where she was; it was not one of us. As if led by a guide he threw himself against the doors of her room with a terrible cry; he bent the bolts out of their sockets, and so forced his way into the room. And there we saw Jocasta, hanging, her neck caught in a swinging noose of rope. When Oedipus saw her he gave a deep dreadful cry of sorrow and loosened the rope round her neck. And when the poor woman was lying on the ground—then we saw the most dreadful sight of all. He ripped out the golden pins with which her clothes were fastened, raised them high above his head, and speared the pupils of his eyes. "You will not see," he said, "the horrors I have suffered and done. Be dark forever now—eyes that saw those you should never have seen, and failed to recognize those you longed to see." Murmuring words like these he raised his hands and struck his eyes again, and again. And each time the wounded eyes sent a stream of blood down his chin, no oozing flow but a dark shower of it, thick as a hailstorm.

These are the sorrows which have burst out and overwhelmed them both, man and wife alike. The wealth and happiness they once had was real while it lasted, but now—weeping, destruction, death, shame—name any shape of evil you will, they have them all.

CHORUS

And Oedipus—poor wretched Oedipus—has he now some rest from pain?

MESSENGER

He is shouting, "Open the doors, someone: show me to all the people of Thebes, my father's killer, my mother's"—I cannot repeat his unholy words. He speaks of banishing himself from Thebes, says he will not remain in his house under the curse which he himself pronounced. But he has no strength: he needs someone to guide his steps. The pain is more than he can bear.

But he will show you himself. The bolts of this door are opening. Now you will see a spectacle that even his enemies would pity.

[*Enter Oedipus from door, blind.*]

CHORUS

O suffering dreadful for mankind to see, most dreadful of all I ever saw. What madness came over you? What unearthly spirit, leaping farther than the mind can conceive, swooped down on your destiny? I pity you. I have many questions to ask you, much I wish to know; my eyes are drawn towards you—but I cannot bear to look. You fill me with horror.

OEDIPUS

Where am I going? Pity me! Where does my voice range to through the air? O spirit, what a leap you made!

CHORUS

To a point of dread, too far for men's ears and eyes.

OEDIPUS

Darkness, dark cloud all around me, enclosing me, unspeakable darkness, irresistible—you came to me on a wind that seemed favorable. Ah, I feel the stab of these sharp pains, and with it the memory of my sorrow.

CHORUS

In such torment it is no wonder that your pain and mourning should be double.

OEDIPUS

My friend! You are by my side still, you alone. You still stay by me, looking after the blind man. I know you are there. I am in the dark, but I can distinguish your voice clearly.

CHORUS

You have done a dreadful thing. How could you bring yourself to put out the light of your eyes? What superhuman power urged you on?

OEDIPUS

It was Apollo, friends, Apollo, who brought to fulfillment all my sufferings. But the hand that struck my eyes was mine and mine alone. What use had I for eyes? Nothing I could see would bring me joy.

96

CHORUS

It was just as you say.

OEDIPUS

What was there for me to look at, to speak to, to love? What joyful word can I expect to hear, my friends? Take me away, out of this country, quickly, take me away. I am lost, accursed, and hated by the gods beyond all other men.

CHORUS

I am moved to pity by your misfortunes and your understanding of them, too. I wish I had never known you!

OEDIPUS

A curse on the man who freed my feet from the cruel bonds on the mountain, who saved me and rescued me from death. He will get no thanks from me. I might have died then and there; but now I am a source of grief for myself and all who love me.

CHORUS

I wish it had turned out that way, too.

OEDIPUS

I would never have become my father's killer, never have been known to all men as my own mother's husband. Now I am godforsaken, the son of an accursed marriage, my own father's successor in the marriage bed. If there is any evil worse than the worst that a man can suffer—Oedipus has drawn it for his lot.

CHORUS

I cannot say you made the right decision. You would have been better dead than blind.

OEDIPUS

What I have done was the best thing to do. Don't read me any more lessons, don't give me any more advice. With what eyes could I have faced my father in the house of the dead, or my poor mother? I have done things to them both for which hanging is too small a punishment.

Do you think I longed to look at my children, born the way they were? No, not with these eyes of mine, never! Not this town either, its walls, its holy temples of the gods. From all of this I am cut off, I, the most nobly raised in Thebes, cut off by my own act. It was I who proclaimed that everyone should expel the impious man—the man the gods have now revealed as unholy—and the son of Laius. After I had exposed my own guilt—and what a guilt! —do you think I could have looked at my fellow citizens with steady eyes?

No, no! If there had been some way to block the source of hearing, I would not have held back: I would have isolated my wretched body completely, so as to see and hear nothing at all. If my mind could be put beyond reach of my miseries— that would be my pleasure.

O Cithaeron, why did you receive me? Why did you not take and kill me on the spot, so that I should never reveal my origin to mankind?

O Polybus, and Corinth, and the ancient house I thought was my father's—what a handsome heir you raised up in me, how rotten beneath the surface! For now I am exposed—evil and born in evil.

O three roads in the deep valley, you oak wood and you narrow pass where the three roads meet, you who soaked up my father's blood, spilled by my hand—do you remember me? Do you remember what I did there, and what I did when I came here?

O marriage, marriage! You gave me birth, and then bred up seed from the one you brought into the world. You made an incestuous breed of father, brother, son—bride, wife, mother—all the most shameful things known to man.

But I must not speak of things that should never have been done. Quickly, in God's name, hide me somewhere outside Thebes, kill me, throw me into the sea, where you will never see me again.

Come close to me. I am a man of sorrow, but take courage and touch me. Do not be afraid; do what I ask. The evil is mine; no one but me can bear its weight.

[*Enter Creon, from side, with attendants.*]

CHORUS LEADER

Here is Creon. He will listen to your request. Decision and action are up to him, now that he has taken your place as the sole ruler of Thebes.

OEDIPUS

What shall I say to him? What justification, what grounds for trust can I present? In everything I did to him before, I have been proved wrong.

CREON

I have not come to mock you, Oedipus, nor to reproach you for the wrong you did.

[*To attendants*] If you have no respect for the feelings of human beings, at least show reverence for the sunlight which nourishes all men. Do not leave him there in full view, an object of dread and horror which appalls the holy rain and the daylight. Get him into the palace as fast as you can.

[*The attendants move over to Oedipus, and stand by him until the end of the scene.*]

Only his family should see the family shame; this public spectacle is indecent.

OEDIPUS

In God's name—since you have exceeded my hopes and come in so generous a spirit to one so low—do something for me. I ask it in your interest, not mine.

CREON

What is it you are so anxious to have me do?

OEDIPUS

Banish me from this country as fast as you can

—to a place where no man can see me or speak to me.

CREON

You can be sure I would have done so already, but first I wanted to ask the god Apollo what should be done.

OEDIPUS

But his command was clear, every word of it; death for the unholy man, the father-killer.

CREON

That *is* what the oracle said. But all the same, in our situation, it is better to inquire what should be done.

OEDIPUS

Will you consult Apollo about anyone as miserable as I?

CREON

Yes, and this time, I take it, you will believe what the god says.

OEDIPUS

Yes. I command you—and beg you—the woman in the palace, see to her burial. She is your sister, you are the man to do this. As for me, do not condemn this city of my fathers to shelter me within its walls, but let me live on the mountain, on Cithaeron, forever linked with my name, the mountain which my mother and father while they still lived chose as my burial place. Let me die there where they tried to kill me.

And yet I know this—no disease or anything else will destroy me. Otherwise I would never have been saved from death in the first place. I was saved —for some strange and dreadful end.

Well, let my destiny go where it will. As for my children, do not concern yourself about the boys, Creon. They are men; and will always find a way to live, wherever they may be. But my two poor helpless girls, who were always at my table, who shared the same food I ate—take care of them for me.

What I wish for most is this. Let me touch them with these hands, as I weep for my sorrows. Please, my lord! Grant my prayer, generous man! If I could hold them I would think I had them with me, as I did when I could see.

[*Antigone and Ismene are led in from the door by a nurse.*]

What's that? I hear something. Oh, God. It is my daughters, weeping. Creon took pity on me, and sent them to me, my dearest ones, my children. Am I right?

CREON

Yes, you are. I did this for you knowing the joy you always took in them, the joy you feel now.

OEDIPUS

Bless you for it! May you be rewarded for sending them. May God watch over you better than He did over me.

Children, where are you? Come here, come to these hands of mine, your brother's hands, the hands that intervened to make your father's once bright eyes so dim. Blind and thoughtless, I became your father, and your mother was my mother, too. I weep for you—see you I cannot—when I think of your future, the bitter life you will lead, the way men will treat you. What gatherings will you go to, what festivals, without returning home in tears, instead of taking part in the ceremonies?

And when you come to the age of marriage, who will take the risk, my daughters, and shoulder the burden of reproach which will be directed at my children—and yours? No reproach is missing. Your father killed his father. He sowed the field from which he himself had sprung, and begot you, his children, at the source of his own being. These are the reproaches you will hear. And who will marry you? There is no one who will do so, children; your destiny is clear—to waste away unmarried, childless.

Creon, you are the only father they have now, for we who brought them into the world are both of us destroyed. Do not abandon them to wander husbandless in poverty: they are your own flesh and blood. Do not make them equal to me and my miserable state, but pity them. They are children, they have no protector but you. Promise me this, noble Creon, touch me with your hand to confirm your promise.

And you, children—if you were old enough to understand, I would have much advice to give you. But as it is, I will tell you what to pray for. Pray that you may find a place where you are allowed to live, and for a life happier than your father's.

CREON

You have wept long enough. Now go inside the house.

OEDIPUS

I must obey, though it gives me no pleasure.

CREON

Yes, everything is good in its proper place and time.

OEDIPUS

I will go in then, but on one condition.

CREON

Tell me what it is. I am listening.

OEDIPUS

You must send me into exile—away from Thebes.

CREON

What you ask for is a gift only Apollo can grant.

OEDIPUS

But I am hateful to the gods above all men.

CREON

In that case, they will grant your request at once.

OEDIPUS

You consent, then?

CREON

It is not my habit to say what I don't mean.

OEDIPUS

Then take me away from here at once.

CREON

Come then, but let go of the children.

OEDIPUS

No, don't take them away from me.

CREON

Don't try to be master in everything. What you once won and held did not stay with you all your life long.

[*The following speech, for reasons too technical to discuss here, is considered by many authorities to be an addition to the play made by a later producer. The translator shares this opinion, but the lines are printed here for those who wish to use them.*]

CHORUS

Citizens who dwell in Thebes, look at Oedipus here, who knew the answer to the famous riddle and was a power in the land. On his good fortune all the citizens gazed with envy. Into what a stormy sea of dreadful trouble he has come now. Therefore we must call no man happy while he waits to see his last day, not until he has passed the border of life and death without suffering pain.

CRITICAL EXCERPTS

1. A perfect tragedy should ... imitate actions which excite pity and fear, this being the distinctive mark of tragic imitation. It follows plainly, in the first place, that the change of fortune presented must not be the spectacle of a virtuous man brought from prosperity to adversity: for this moves neither pity nor fear; it merely shocks us. Nor, again, that of a bad man passing from adversity to prosperity, for nothing can be more alien to the spirit of Tragedy: it possesses no single tragic quality; it neither satisfies the moral sense nor calls forth pity or fear. Nor, again, should the downfall of the utter villain be exhibited. A plot of this kind would, doubtless, satisfy the moral sense, but it would inspire neither pity nor fear; for pity is aroused by unmerited misfortune, fear by the misfortune of a man like ourselves. Such an event, therefore, will be neither pitiful nor terrible. There remains, then, the character between these two extremes—that of a man who is not eminently good and just, yet whose misfortune is brought about not by vice or

depravity, but by some error or frailty. He must be one who is highly renowned and prosperous—a personage like Oedipus. . . .

Reversal of the situation is a change by which the action veers round to its opposite, subject always to our rule of probability or necessity. Thus in the *Oedipus,* the messenger comes to cheer Oedipus and free him from his alarms about his mother, but by revealing who he is, he produces the opposite effect. . . .

Recognition, as the name indicates, is a change from ignorance to knowledge, producing love or hate between the persons destined by the poet for good or bad fortune. The best form of recognition is coincident with a Reversal of the Situation, as in the *Oedipus.* . . .

But, of all recognitions, the best is that which arises from the incidents themselves, where the startling discovery is made by natural means. Such is that in the *Oedipus* of Sophocles.

Fear and pity may be aroused by spectacular means; but they may also result from the inner structure of the piece, which is the better way, and indicates a superior poet. For the plot ought to be so constructed that, even without the aid of the eye, he who hears the tale told will thrill with horror and melt to pity at what takes place. This is the impression we should receive from hearing the story of the *Oedipus.* . . .

The Poetics of Aristotle,
translated by S. H. Butcher,
Macmillan, 1902

2. The *Oedipus Rex* is a tragedy of fate: its tragic effect depends on the conflict between the all-powerful will of the gods and the vain efforts of human beings threatened with disaster; resignation to the divine will, and the perception of one's own impotence is the lesson which the deeply moved spectator is supposed to learn from the tragedy. Modern authors have therefore sought to achieve a similar tragic effect by expressing the same conflict in stories of their own invention. But the playgoers have looked on unmoved . . . The modern tragedies of destiny have failed of their effect. If the *Oedipus Rex* is capable of moving a modern reader or playgoer no less powerfully than it moved the contemporary Greeks, the only possible explanation is that the effect of the Greek tragedy does not depend upon the conflict between fate and human will, but upon the peculiar nature of the material by which this conflict is revealed. There must be a voice within us which is prepared to acknowledge the compelling power of fate in the *Oedipus,* . . . this [Oedipus'] fate moves us only because it might have been our own, because the oracle laid upon us before our birth the very curse which rested upon him. It may be that we were all destined to direct our first sexual impulses toward our mothers and our first impulses of hatred and violence toward our fathers; our dreams convince us that we were.

"The Interpretation of Dreams," in
The Basic Writings of Sigmund Freud,
Random House, 1938

3. This famous passage is, of course, a landmark in the history of modern thought, and it is a token of the vitality of Greek literature that in these sentences one of the most bitterly contested and influential concepts of the modern mind takes the form of an attempt to solve a critical problem raised by the Sophoclean play. But quite apart from the value (or lack of it) of Freud's theory of the Oedipus complex (which he here announced for the first time), the solution he proposes to the critical problem raised by calling the play a "tragedy of fate" cannot be accepted. When he says that Oedipus' fate affects us because "it might have been our own" he has put his finger on an essential aspect of the tragedy, the universality of the theme, which of course extends far beyond the particular appeal which Freud himself here expounds. But the universal appeal of the theme, whether understood in psychoanalytical or other terms, does not explain the dramatic excitement generated by the tragedy. No amount of symbolic richness—conscious, subconscious, or unconscious—will create dramatic excitement in a play which does not possess the essential prerequisites of human free will and responsibility. The tragedy must be self-sufficient: that is, the catastrophe must be the result of the free decision and action (or inaction) of the tragic protagonist.

The problem, stated in Freud's terms (and he only states in extreme form what many others imply or assume), is obviously insoluble. If the *Oedipus Tyrannus* is a "tragedy of fate," the hero's will is not free, and the dramatic efficiency of the play is limited by that fact. The problem is insoluble; but luckily the problem does not exist to start with. For in the play which Sophocles wrote, the hero's will is absolutely free and he is fully responsible for the catastrophe.

Oedipus at Thebes,
Bernard Knox

4. [Oedipus'] . . . humiliation is a lesson both to others and to him. Democritus's words, "the foolish learn modesty in misfortune," may be applied to Oedipus, who has indeed been foolish in his mistakes and illusions and has been taught modesty through suffering.

Sophoclean Tragedy,
C. M. Bowra,
Oxford University Press, 1944

5. Oedipus *tyrannos,* then, is more than an individual tragic hero. In his title, *tyrannos,* in the nature and basis of his power, in his character, and in the mode of his dramatic action, he resembles Athens, the city which aimed to become (and was already far along the road to becoming) the *tyrannos* of Greece, the rich and splendid autocrat of the whole Hellenic world. Such a resemblance, whether consciously recognized or not, must have won him the sympathy of the Athenian audience and firmly engaged the emotions of that audience in the hero's action and suffering. But it does something more. It adds an extra dimension of significance not only to his career but also to his fall,

which suggests, in symbolic, prophetic, riddling terms, the fall of Athens itself. Like Oedipus, Athens justifies unceasing and ever more vigorous action by an appeal to previous success; like Oedipus, Athens refuses to halt, to compromise, to turn back; like Oedipus, Athens follows the dictates of her energy and intelligence with supreme confidence in the future; and like Oedipus, the tragedy seems to suggest, Athens will come to know defeat, learn to say "I must obey" as she now says "I must rule." Athens, in the words of her greatest statesman, claimed that she was an example to others . . . Oedipus is called an example too, but in his fall.

Oedipus at Thebes,
Bernard Knox

6. It sometimes happens that a great poet creates a character in whom the essence of an age is distilled, a representative figure who in his action and suffering presents to his own time the image of its victory and defeat. For later centuries this character becomes the central reference point for an understanding of his creator's time; but he is a figure of such symbolic potency that he appears to them not only as a historical but also as a contemporary phenomenon. The poet who created him has penetrated so deeply into the permanent elements of the human situation that his creation transcends time. One such figure is Hamlet, Prince of Denmark, and such another is Oedipus, King of Thebes. . . .

Oedipus is symbolic of all human achievement: his hard-won magnificence, unlike the everlasting magnificence of the divine, cannot last, and while it lives, shines all the more brilliant against the somber background of its impermanency. Sophocles' tragedy presents us with a terrible affirmation of man's subordinate position in the universe, and at the same time with a heroic vision of man's victory in defeat. Man is not equated to the gods, but man at his greatest, as in Oedipus, is capable of something which the gods, by definition, cannot experience; the proud tragic view of Sophocles sees in the fragility and inevitable defeat of human greatness the possibility of a purely human heroism to which the gods can never attain, for the condition of their existence is everlasting victory.

Oedipus at Thebes,
Bernard Knox,
Yale University Press, 1957

7. Professor Waldock, who writes with refreshing good sense about the plays and their problems, objects to the notion that great plays must contain profound truths, or even "mean something"; to him *Œdipus Rex* is simply a wonderful story, rather than a universal situation. The whole uncertainty about the "meaning" of these plays would seem to indicate that their greatness does not depend on any specific meaning. Yet Sophocles was manifestly a thoughtful writer, concerned with major issues of human conduct and human destiny. Almost all readers feel that his plays

positively do "mean something"—that he was expressing, however obliquely, some "philosophy of life." And almost all commentators agree on certain qualities that are clues to his thought, notably his irony and his refusal to declare himself in so many words. In our own world these might imply a devotion to art for art's sake. In the Greek world they imply a measure of philosophical skepticism. Sophocles was at least saying that the ways of deity are mysterious, and often painfully so.

> *The Spirit of Tragedy,*
> Herbert J. Muller,
> Washington Square Press, 1965

8. . . . the Greek theatre was religious, not commercial . . . What the Greeks wrote were, from our point of view, not much more than long one-act plays: they take little over an hour, at most an hour and a half, to perform . . . a chorus that sings and dances is found in all works written by major playwrights. The reader must keep in mind, must remember that the serious plays were part grand opera and the comedies part musicals.

> *Classical Age,*
> Lionel Casson, Editor,
> Dell Publishing Co., 1965

9. Now, why is it that today, when no man alive believes in Apollo or worries about the Delphic ora-

cle, lovers of literature still find themselves involved in Oedipus' problems and his personality? Obviously Sophocles deals here with a universal situation that transcends the interests and circumstances of fifth-century B.C. Athens. Oedipus is a symbolic figure for all mankind.

Most significant to us, perhaps, is Oedipus' noble assumption of full responsibility for his own past. In an obvious sense, his troubles have been caused by Laius and Jocasta's blind way of handling their problems, by the shepherd's failure to obey orders, by Polybus and Merope's unwillingness to tell him the truth. Yet Oedipus recognizes that each man is an embodiment of his own heritage and must accept the consequences of his own personality, even if he did not create that personality all by himself.

Secondly, we all operate, most of the time, in partial ignorance of the full situation. We are all, at any time, liable to discover that we have oversimplified. We are all in danger of assuming that because we defeated one Sphinx, we can defeat all Sphinxes. Oedipus appalls us, and we identify with him because he illustrates the ridiculously conflicting demands made on man. He must act as if he knows what he is doing when he cannot possibly be sure of ultimate causes or effects.

Thirdly, like Oedipus, we all suffer some difficulties with the older generation, with authority figures. It is inevitable—as children grow up and test out their own powers—that there be some conflict of interest with their parents. Oedipus' fears that he may hurt his parents find an echo in everyone who wants to be strong and independent, yet sensitive and fair.

Fourthly, we all identify with Oedipus' passionate drive to know more about his own nature. To what extent is our life determined by heredity, environment, body chemistry, instinct, and the ultimate forces in the universe? To what extent can anybody enjoy free will? To what extent are we too the children of Chance? Puny in the reaches of time and space, situated vaguely midway between the atoms and the stars, like Oedipus, we want to understand the relationship between our finite world and the infinity beyond. We can accept Apollo and Delphi as symbols of the Ultimate Reality and Oedipus as symbolizing man's drive to know his part in the scheme of things.

> "Character Analysis," *Oedipus the King,*
> Walter James Miller,
> Washington Square Press, 1967

10. The plot of the *Oedipus Rex* is a search for knowledge, and its climax is a recognition of truth; the hero is a man whose self-esteem is rooted in his pride of intellect; and the gods, those ever-present figures in tragedy, rarely seen but always essential, manifest themselves here not by thunderbolt or epiphany or sudden madness or miracle, but by a prediction after long delay proved true. Various formulas have been imposed on this play, according to the preferences of various critics. Some of these, like "A wicked man is punished" or "An imprudent man pays the price" have been based on a misreading of facts. Others, like

"A family curse returns" or "An innocent man is victimized by fate" have involved a misjudgment of the play's central concern. Better to call the play "A man matches wits with the gods." Formulas should not be unduly honored, but this one, I think, has the advantage of being suited to Sophocles' play. All of the others remain possible interpretations of the Oedipus legend and nothing more. That is, they sum up plays that might have been written by an author who used the principal facts of that legend as dramatic content.

"A man matches wits with the gods." We have to consider whether we can drop the indefinite article and raise the "m" in "man" to upper case. The main objections will come from those who stress the extraordinary particularity of what Oedipus does and suffers and suppose that this precludes any universal reference. One can begin to meet these objections by observing that the word "knowledge" is ambiguous as it applies to Oedipus. The knowledge he claims to have is the ability to solve riddles. Its connotations are mastery and power—the slain Sphinx, the throne of Thebes, and now perhaps the removal of the plague. On the other hand, the self-knowledge he achieves during the play has quite opposite implications. The ears of Athenians of the late fifth century would have been far better attuned than our own to this contrast. They were familiar with the controversial humanistic conception that man's knowledge, especially his technological and scientific knowledge, constituted his chief protection against disaster and his claim to greatness. That is a datum in the history of Greek language and culture. Consequently, the posture Oedipus adopts before his fall, though it has been self-explanatory in all ages, belongs to a *type* of attitude especially familiar to them. On the other hand, his discovery of his own identity would also have had rather clearer associations in Sophocles' time than it does now. The play makes it evident that for Oedipus, if for no one else, self-knowledge is an appalling and a humbling experience. There is at first sight no universal meaning discernible here: Oedipus has had a singular past to learn about, and there will always be readers to say that this has nothing to do with them. But it would have reminded any Greek spectator of the maxim engraved at Delphi, which was attributed to more than one of the Seven Wise Men and had become a part of the popular wisdom: Know Thyself. There was, moreover, a commonly accepted way of understanding the phrase, viz. "Know your limitations, especially in relation to the gods, and stay within them." Self-knowledge is therefore understandably associated with the virtue of *sophrosyne,* a word usually best translated as modesty or self-restraint. The closer we look at the way Sophocles has organized his play, the less remote the story of Oedipus comes to seem from common Greek and common human concerns. As a man who in the flush of past achievement and present challenge seems to have cast off the burden of his human limitations and is then suddenly crushed under them, Oedipus is an example, however extreme, of what may happen to anyone. The chorus recognizes this immediately: "Having your example (*paradeigma*), your fate, O wretched Oedipus, I count nothing mortal blessed." In their eyes, at this extraordinarily important moment in the play, Oedipus is not primarily their king or their suffering friend (they will come to these points later) but an example (*paradeigma*) of all mankind.

Twentieth Century Interpretations of Oedipus Rex,
Michael J. O'Brien, Editor

11. Throughout the play, no matter what is happening, whatever may be the actual intentions, desires, and assumptions of the various characters, whatever they say, in anger, triumph, depression, or alarm, one great thought is kept always before the *audience:* none of the people involved (except the blind prophet and the old shepherd, of course) has the faintest idea of the one hideous truth, the truth that drains all significance from what they are doing or saying. It is this vision, given only to the audience, that unifies the diverse actions and gives the play its celebrated concentration—the feeling that it is all one tremendous thrust, without subplot or elaboration, without a single superfluous scene or speech. Many things *seem* to be happening, but only one thing is really happening. Sophocles achieves this effect in two ways. First, he brings Oedipus face to face with all the evidence again and again, only to show him discovering expla-

nations and hypotheses that are far more reasonable and sensible than the truth. (This is hardly a fault in the structure of the play, as Voltaire and others have thought. It is what keeps the audience focused on the real issue.) Second, all the players, even the elders, say things that are natural and to the point, given what they understand, but which simultaneously remind the audience of the terrible distance between reality and their comprehension of it. We are given a double vision, then: the false one, on the human level, complex and confused, and the true one on the divine level, appallingly simple in its action.

> *Oedipus the King,*
> Thomas Gould,
> Prentice-Hall, 1970

12. At the center of the drama is Oedipus with his absolute determination to know the truth. He dominates from beginning to end. The paradox which divides interpreters and renders the play so perpetually fascinating is how the mind of Oedipus both succeeds and fails. The work proves how frail mortals are; all his energy and skill have only brought him ruin, and the chorus takes him as an example of why nothing in the world can be called blessed. The prophet is right in saying that skill at riddles ruined him. Yet this response to the claim of Oedipus to be great in this above all does not cancel what Oedipus has said, and Oedipus also claims not to care if his skill ruined himself, since he saved Thebes. Both the errors of the search and the final discovery display

the limits of human ability, but Oedipus does at least find the truth he seeks.

In the scene with the herdsman, Oedipus evidently knows before the final word is spoken. The very struggle of the slave to avoid telling what he knows reveals how dreadful it is. Oedipus here is angry for the last time in the play, and his anger is again directed at one who withholds the truth from him. But this time, as he is closer to ruin he is also far closer to truth, and his anger attains its goal. When Oedipus threatens to torture the old man, the point is not his cruelty but his rage to learn what he realizes is a terrible truth. When at last the slave cries out that he is on the verge of horror and about to declare it, Oedipus replies almost gently: "And I of hearing. But still I must hear." Oedipus insists on the truth, and in winning the truth in some sense makes it his own.

Sophocles,
Ruth Scodel,
Twayne Publishers, 1984

13. The dramatist is a performance artist who manipulates real bodies in real space on the stage, but he is also a poet/writer who fashions myths into stories about passions, with the freedom of his plastic medium of words. Sophocles worked with the visible, public space of the open-air theater of Dionysus to reveal truths about hidden or invisible areas of existence that his poetry could call up in the imagination. Although the publicly enacted dimension of this art

form was the most important to its original audience, who responded to it primarily as theater, its more private, psychological dimension remains rich with insights for the modern reader, who is more likely to approach these works as written texts.

Oedipus Tyrannus is above all a great drama, but it also contains hints of the poet's awareness of the problem of representing reality, and especially the inner reality of the emotional life. This concern is particularly present in Sophocles' attention to what is shown and what is seen in the climactic scene of Oedipus' discovery of the buried truth, followed by his display of himself from the hitherto hidden interior of the palace. Revealing to an audience what is concealed behind doors and gates—the gates of the palace, of the mouth, or of the body—is not only a matter of practical dramaturgy. It is also the poet's reflection on the way that his art probes the dark side of life and the hidden depths of the soul, and on the way that our fascination with the spectacle makes us, like Oedipus, see what we would rather not see and know what we would prefer not to know.

Oedipus Tyrannus,
Charles Segal,
Twayne Publishers, 1993

SUGGESTIONS FOR FURTHER READING

Alister Cameron. *The Identity of Oedipus the King*. New York: New York University Press, 1968.

Diskin Clay. Introduction to *Sophocles' Oedipus the King*. Translated by Stephen Berg and Diskin Clay. New York: Oxford University Press, 1978.

Thomas Gould. *Oedipus the King. Translated with Commentary*. Englewood Cliffs, N.J.: Prentice-Hall, 1970.

Gordon M. Kirkwood. *A Study of Sophoclean Drama*. Ithaca: Cornell University Press, 1958.

Bernard Knox. *Oedipus at Thebes*. 2nd edition. New Haven: Yale University Press, 1966.

_____ . "The Freedom of Oedipus." In *Essays Ancient and Modern*. Baltimore: Johns Hopkins University Press, 1989.

Richard Lattimore. *The Poetry of Greek Tragedy*. Baltimore: Johns Hopkins University Press, 1958. New York: Harper & Row, 1966.

SUGGESTIONS FOR FURTHER READING

Michael J. O'Brien, editor. *Twentieth Century Interpretations of Oedipus Rex*. Englewood Cliffs, N.J.: Prentice-Hall, 1968.

Ruth Scodel. *Sophocles*. Boston: Twayne Publishers, 1984.

Charles Segal. *Oedipus Tyrannus: Tragic Heroism and the Limits of Knowledge*. New York: Twayne Publishers, 1993.

_____ . *Tragedy and Civilization: An Interpretation of Sophocles*. Cambridge: Harvard University Press, 1981.

Cedric Whitman. *Sophocles: A Study of Heroic Humanism*. Cambridge: Harvard University Press, 1951.

R. P. Winnington-Ingram. *Sophocles: An Interpretation*. New York: Cambridge University Press, 1980.